Alexander Taylor

DAY TRADING GUIDE

Master Day Trading for a Living and create Your Passive Income with a positive ROI in 19 days. Learn all Strategies, Tools for Money Management, Discipline and Trader Psychology

TABLE OF CONTENTS

Introduction

Before the advent of computers, only those people were involved in trading who had direct access to stock markets. These were mostly from financial institutions, trading houses, or brokerage houses. Short-term trading was considered gambling; day trading was not popular in those days, and stock markets were meant only for long term investing.

Once the internet became accessible to common people, day trading or short-term trading also rose in popularity. Online trading and brokerage houses emerged quickly and attracted a large customer base. The convenience of accessing stock markets from one's home; or sitting in a cafe, created a new, lucrative career for or those who were interested in financial markets. Suddenly investors became an old-fashioned word, and day trading became the buzzword.

With the rising popularity and concept of making money by just sitting at a desk, came some misconceptions. Before we proceed further into the mechanism of daily trading, we must clear these misconceptions.

Day trading is NOT some get-rich-quick scheme:

The biggest fascination, and the misconception, about everyday trading is that it is a money generating machine. It is not. People mistakenly assume that all you have to do is buy and sell every day, and you will be making big profits. This kind of thinking leads to huge losses for retail traders, who blindly jump into stock markets, listen to the advice of their friends, colleagues, TV experts, or even seamstress, and eventually lose their shirt. Trading in financial markets requires a thorough knowledge of the functioning of these entities, a disciplined approach, and considerable patience. Do not make the mistake of imagining day trading as easy as playing a lottery or gambling in the casinos. Money making, in any business, is not dependent on luck or chance. It is a calculated risk, which is taken after meticulous research of that field of business and knowledge. If you wish to enter the arena of day trading, make it your career, and earn your living by it, then learn its intricacies. Study all those aspects that impact the results of day trading. Take a step-by-step approach for acquiring the necessary skill sets to finally become a successful day trader.

After all, when you are spending money to earn money, you cannot afford to be unsuccessful in that venture.

Day trading is NOT a 9 to 5 job:

Another common misconception that causes a loss for many retail traders is that day trading is like their 9-to-5 job. They assume; you start trading as soon as markets open (reaching the workplace at a fixed time), trade through the day, and close your trades when the closing bell rings (leave the work workplace at a fixed hour). Workings of financial markets are not like a steady desk job. A plethora of factors that affect the functioning of financial markets and their entities, such as stocks, commodities, currencies, and indices. These are all instruments of day trading and are influenced by the happenings in business, finance, and geopolitical events. There is a very common term related to trading. It is called "market volatility." This term denotes the fluctuation in financial markets. While there are hardly any "fluctuations" or rapid changes in any 9-to-5 desk job, in the world of trading fluctuations happen in seconds! This volatility can be stomach-churning for new traders. One can only master these volatile fluctuations in stock markets by having an in-depth knowledge of how markets function and learning to use this volatility for trading. Remember, when you begin day trading, you put your money at risk. Your purpose should be to obtain every bit of knowledge, which will decrease this risk and improve the chances of reward.

CHAPTER 1:

How Day Trading Works

A lways keep the primary rule of day trading in mind: never hold on to a position overnight, even if it means taking a loss on trades.

But why do you have to stick to this rule even if it means suffering trading losses? After all, isn't making money the point of day trading?

Yes, making money is the point of day trading. But given that the ideal securities to day trade are volatile ones, holding on to them overnight can put you at high risk for more significant losses the next day. It's ok to take small losses on day trades than large ones when you try to holding day trading securities overnight in the hopes that prices will recover significantly the next day.

By closing your position at the end of the day, even at a loss, you get to minimize day trading losses. And if you close positions at a profit, awesome! Don't feel like you could earn more by waiting until tomorrow. Remember, a bird in the hand's better than three in the bush.

You'll also need to remember that trading is a lot different than regular investing. While trading is a form of investing, regular investing usually refers to a more passive, buying-and-holding strategy that waits for months and years before taking profits. Trading has a much shorter time frame, which is only several hours for day trading and a couple of months at most for swing trading.

Buying Long and Selling Short

When you buy financial security, you take a long position on that security. When you hear a trader say that he or she's long 100 shares Intel stocks, it means that the trader bought and is currently holding a hundred shares of Intel's stocks.

The point of taking a long position on financial security is selling them later on at higher prices. To close a long position, you sell the securities you're holding.

When you sell securities that you don't own yet, you take a short position on that security. When you hear a trader say he or she shorted or sold short 100 shares of Intel stocks, it means that the trader sold 100 shares of Intel stocks, hoping that its price will continue dropping so he or she can repurchase it at a much lower price. It's the same principle as buying low and selling high, except that the "selling high" part comes before the "buying low" part.

How can you sell something you don't have, and more importantly, why would you even do that?

First, let's answer why you should do that? And the answer is: to make money when prices of securities are dropping. As mentioned earlier, it's just a reversal of the general trading strategy of buying securities at low prices and selling them at higher ones. By selling securities while their prices are high and buying them later on at lower prices, you can trade profitably even during market downturns.

Now, how can you do it? Depending on your broker and whether you're qualified, you can borrow the securities from your broker, sell them, repurchase them when prices drop, and return the securities you acquired from your broker. In the process, you profit from the short sell.

Keep in mind, however, that just like taking long positions, short selling also has its risks, which include that prices may actually go up instead of continuing to go down. In that case, you may also suffer trading losses.

You may be wondering, why would brokers or exchanges lend securities to their clients for short selling instead of selling the securities themselves? That's an excellent question. And the answer is: brokers usually want to take long term positions on securities. Why?

Why take risks with short-term trades on a downward trending market when they can make money with much lower risks by merely lending it to customers who want to short sell for a fee. This way, everybody wins. The long-term investors get to keep their securities and profit, even during bear markets, while those who don't own securities can have opportunities to make profitable trades via short-selling.

Retail vs. Institutional Traders

Retail traders are individuals who can be either part-time or full traders but don't work for a firm and are not managing funds from other people. These traders hold a small percentage of the volume in the trade market.

On the other hand, institutional traders are composed of hedge funds, mutual funds, and investment banks that are often armed with advanced software and are usually engaged in high-frequency trading.

Nowadays, human involvement is quite minimal in the operations of investment firms. Backed up by professional analysts and huge investments, institutional investors can be quite aggressive.

So, at this point, you might be wondering how a beginner like you can compete against the big players?

Our advantage is the freedom and flexibility we enjoy. Institutional traders have the legal obligation to trade. Meanwhile, individual traders are free to trade or to take a break from trading if the market is currently unstable.

Institutional traders should be active in the market and trade huge volumes of stocks, regardless of the stock price. Individual traders are free to sit out and trade if there are possible opportunities in the market.

But sadly, most retail traders do not possess the know-how in identifying the right time to be active and the best time to wait. If you want to be profitable in day trading, you need to eliminate greed and develop patience.

The biggest problem of losers in day trading is not the size of their accounts or the lack of access to technology, but their sheer lack of discipline. Many are prone to bad money management and over-trading.

Some retail traders are successful by following the guerilla strategy, which refers to the unconventional approach to trading derived from guerilla warfare. Guerilla combatants are skilled in using hit-and-run tactics like raids, sabotage, and ambushes to manipulate a more prominent and less-mobile conventional opponent.

Remember, your mission is not to defeat institutional traders. Instead, you should focus on waiting for the right opportunity to earn your target income.

As a retail trader, you can make profits from market volatility. It can be impossible to make money if the markets are flat. Only institutional traders have the tools, expertise, and money to gamble in such circumstances.

You must learn how to choose stocks that can help you make fast decisions to the downside or upside in a predictable approach. On the other hand, institutional traders follow high-frequency trading, which allows them to profit from minimal price movements.

But for a brief overview, Alpha Predators are what retail traders are hunting for. These stocks usually tank when the markets are running, and they run when the markets are tanking.

It is generally okay if the market is running, and the stocks are running as well. Just be sure that you are trading stocks that are moving because they have a valid reason to move and are not just moving with the general market conditions.

Probably, you are wondering what the necessary catalyst for stocks is to make them ideal for day trading.

Here are some catalysts:

- Debt offerings

- Buybacks

- Stock splits

- Management changes

- Layoffs

- Restructuring

- Significant contract wins/losses

- Partnerships/alliances

- Major product releases

- Mergers and/or acquisitions

- FDA approval/disapproval

- Earnings surprises

- Earnings reports

Retail traders who are engaged in reversal trades usually choose stocks that are selling off because there has been some bad press about the company. Whenever there's a fast sell-off because of bad press, many traders will notice and begin monitoring the stock for what is called a bottom reversal.

How can you identify the stocks that are alluring retail traders? There are some proven ways to do this.

First, you can use day trading stock scanners. Basically, the stocks that are significantly moving up or down are the stocks that are being monitored by retail traders.

Second, find online community groups or social media groups where retail traders hang out. Twitter and Stock Twits are often good places to learn what is currently trending. If you regularly follow successful traders, then you may see for yourself what everyone is following. There's a significant advantage to being part of a community of day traders.

Securities in Play

There's a reason why many investors, traders, and analysts focus on market movements or indices. It's because they know that, for the most part, most financial securities follow the overall trend of their respective markets unless they have an excellent reason not to. For example, the prices of most stocks in the NYSE tend to go up when the Dow Jones is trending upwards and vice versa.

However, there will always be outliers that will – for one reason or another – go against the general trend for some specific purpose. When their general markets are tanking, they're picking up. When their general markets are picking up, their tanking.

These securities are called securities in play (SIP). As a retail or individual day trader, these are the securities you should focus on within your chosen day trading market.

If you want to day trade stocks, these are stocks that buck the general trend of the NYSE or the NASDAQ. If futures contract, these will be futures contracts that go against the general direction of most other similar agreements.

You get the drift, right? Right!

What are some of the reasons that may account for the contrarian behavior of SIPs? These may include:

Unexpected results of earnings;

Surprise company or economic developments; and Major policy changes by the governing authorities.

So, just because a particular security bucks its general market trend doesn't mean you can consider it a SIP. There should be an underlying reason for the contrarian movement. If none, it's probably not a SIP.

Always remember another important day trading rule, particularly for choosing SIPs to day trade: Find out if a particular security's movement is due to general market sentiment or is it due to some unique fundamental reason?

For this, you'll need to do your homework. As a beginner day trader, you may have to do a bit more research than what you're accustomed to. But as you become a more experienced day trader, you'll be able to easily distinguish when a particular security is just going with the general market flow or when it's trending based on a unique and specific reason.

Professional day traders are those who do this type of trading for a living. While other forms of trading can sometimes be done as a hobby or a gambling high, day trading is often not included here. If you don't have a good understanding of the market and its fundamentals, you will most likely lose money.

CHAPTER 2:

How to Think Like an Expert Trader

Know when to go off book: While sticking to your plan, even when your emotions are telling you to ignore it, is the mark of a successful trader, this in no way means that you must blindly follow your plan 100 percent of the time. You will, without a doubt, find yourself in a situation from time to time where your plan is going to be rendered completely useless by something outside of your control. You need to be aware enough of your plan's weaknesses, as well as changing market conditions, to know when following your predetermined course of action is going to lead to failure instead of success. Knowing when the situation really is changing versus when your emotions are trying to hold sway is something that will come with practice, but even being aware of the disparity is a huge step in the right direction.

Avoid trades that are out of the money: While there are a few strategies out there that make it a point of picking up options that are currently out of the money, you can rest assured that they are most certainly the exception, not the rule. Remember, the options market is not like the traditional stock market, which means that even if you are trading options based on underlying stocks buying low and selling high is just not a viable strategy. If a call has dropped out of the money, there is generally less than a 10 percent chance that it will return to acceptable levels before it expires, which means that if you purchase these types of options what you are doing is little better than gambling, and you can find ways to gamble with odds in your favor of much higher than 10 percent.

Avoid hanging on too tightly to your starter strategy: That doesn't mean that it is the last strategy that you are ever going to need, however, far from it. Your core trading strategy is one that should always be constantly evolving as the circumstances surrounding your trading habits change and evolves as well. What's more, outside of your primary strategy you are going to want to eventually create additional plans that are more specifically tailored to various market states or specific strategies that are only useful in a narrow band of situations. Remember, the more prepared you are prior to starting a day's worth of trading, the greater your overall profit level is likely to be, it is as simple as that.

Utilize the spread: If you are not entirely risk averse, then when it comes to taking advantage of volatile trades it's the best thing to do is utilize a spread as a way of both safeguarding your existing investments and, at the same time, making a profit. To utilize a long spread you are going to want to generate a call and a put, both with the same underlying asset, expiration details, and share amounts but with two very different strike prices. The call will need to have a higher strike price and will mark the upper limit of your profits, and the put will have a lower strike price that will mark the lower limit of your losses. When creating a spread it is important that you purchase both halves at the same time as doing it in fits and spurts can add extraneous variables to the formula that are difficult to adjust for properly.

Never proceed without knowing the mood of the market: While using a personalized trading plan is always the right choice, having one doesn't change the fact that it is extremely important to consider the mood of the market before moving forward with the day's trades. First and foremost, it is important to keep in mind that the collective will of all of the traders who are currently participating in the market is just as much as a force as anything that is more concrete, including market news. In fact, even if companies release good news to various outlets and the news is not quite as good as everyone was anticipating it to be, then related prices can still decrease.

To get a good idea of what the current mood of the market is like, you are going to want to know the average daily numbers that are common for your market and be on the lookout for them to start dropping sharply. While a day or two of major fluctuation can be completely normal, anything longer than that is a sure sign that something is up. Additionally, you will always want to be aware of what the major players in your market are up to.

Never get started without a clear plan for entry and exit: While finding your first set of entry/exit points can be difficult without experience to guide you, it is extremely important that you have them locked down prior to starting trading, even if the stakes are relatively low. Unless you are extremely lucky, starting without a clear idea of the playing field is going to do little but lose your money. If you aren't sure about what limits you should set, start with a generalized pair of points and work to fine tune it from there.

More important than setting entry and exit points, however, is using them, even when there is still the appearance of money on the table. One of the biggest hurdles that new options traders need to get over is the idea that you need to wring every last cent out of each and every successful trade. The fact of the matter is that, as long as you have a profitable trading plan, and then there will always be more profitable trades in the future, which mean that instead of worrying about a small extra profit, you should be more concerned with protecting the profit that the trade has already netted you. While you may occasionally make some extra profit ignoring this advice, odds are you will lose far more than you gain as profits peak unexpectedly and begin dropping again before you can effectively pull the trigger. If you are still having a hard time with this concept, consider this: options trading are a marathon, not a sprint, slow and steady will always win the race.

Never double down: When they are caught up in the heat of the moment, many new options traders will find themselves in a scenario where the best way to recoup a serious loss is to double down on the underlying stock in question at its newest, significantly lowered, price in an effort to make a profit under the assumption that things are going to turn around and then continue to do so to the point that everything is completely profitable once again. While it can be difficult to let an underlying stock that was once extremely profitable go, doubling down is rarely, if ever, going to be the correct decision.

If you find yourself in a spot where you don't know if the trade you are about to make is actually going to be a good choice, all you need to do is ask yourself if you would make the same one if you were going into the situation blind, the answer should tell you all you need to know.

If you find yourself in a moment where doubling down seems like the right choice, you are going to need to have the strength to talk yourself back down off of that investing ledge and to cut your losses as thoroughly as possible given the current situation. The sooner you cut your losses and move on from the trade that ended poorly, the sooner you can start putting energy and investments into a trade that still has the potential to make you a profit.

Never take anything personally: It is human nature to build stories around, and therefore form relationships with all manner of inanimate objects, including individual stocks or currency pairs. This is why it is perfectly natural to feel a closer connection to particular trades and possibly even consider throwing out your plan when one of them takes an unexpected dive. Thinking about and acting on are two very different things, however, which is why being aware of these tendencies in order to avoid them at all costs.

This scenario happens just as frequently with trades moving in positive directions as it does negative, but the results are always going to be the same. Specifically, it can be extremely tempting to hang on to a given trade much longer than you might otherwise decide to simply because it is on a hot streak that shows no sign of stopping. In these instances, the better choice of action is to instead sell off half of your shares and then set a new target based on the updated information to ensure you are in a position to have your cake and eat it too.

Not taking your choice of broker seriously: With so many things to consider, it is easy to understand why many new option traders simply settle on the first broker that they find and go about their business from there. The fact of the matter is, however, that the broker you choose is going to be a huge part of your overall trading experience, which means that the importance of choosing the right one should not be discounted if you are hoping for the best experience possible. This means that the first thing that you are going to want to do is to dig past the friendly exterior of their website and get to the meat and potatoes of what it is they truly offer. Remember, creating an eye-catching website is easy, filling it will legitimate information when you have ill intent is much more difficult.

First things first, this means looking into their history of customer service as a way of not only ensuring that they treat their customers in the right way, but also of checking to see that quality of service is where it needs to be as well. Remember, when you make a trade every second count, which means that if you need to contact your broker for help with a trade, you need to know that you are going to be speaking with a person who can solve your problem as quickly as possible. The best way to ensure the customer service is up to snuff is to give them a call and see how long it takes for them to get back to you. If you wait more than a single business day, take your business elsewhere as if they are this disinterested in a new client, consider what the service is going to be like when they already have you right where they want you.

With that out the way, the next thing you will need to consider is the fees that the broker is going to charge in exchange for their services. There is very little regulation when it comes to these fees, which means it is definitely going to pay to shop around. In addition to fees, it is important to consider any account minimums that are required as well as any fees having to do with withdrawing funds from the account.

Find a Mentor: When you are looking to go from causal trader to someone who trades successfully on the regular, there is only so much you can learn by yourself before you need a truly objective eye to ensure you are proceeding appropriately. This person can be someone you know in real life, or it can take the form of one or more people online. The point is you need to find another person or two who you can bounce ideas off of and whose experience you can benefit from. Options trading don't need to be a solitary activity; take advantage of any community you can find.

CHAPTER 3:

Getting Ready for Your Day Trading Career

Welcome to the beginning of the rest of your life. This is the chapter where we talk about how to get your life ready for becoming a day trader, organizing everything you need to get yourself off to the best possible start. This will be a rather lengthy chapter because there's a lot to cover, including making sure you're cut out to be a trader, setting up your trading space, getting your finances in order, and getting ready to go. Here we go.

Is Day Trading Right for You?

This is an important question you need to ask yourself.

Using the questions detailed above, you need to make sure you're going to be committed to becoming a day trader. You must understand you're going to be working long hours, and you don't precisely get holiday breaks since you're your own boss and you're working for yourself.

You will also need to make sure you're not an emotionally reactive kind of person. It's absolutely guaranteed that at some point during your career, you're going to invest in a stock, and you're going to lose money on it. That's just the way the game works, and it's inevitable.

However, if you're an emotional person and you lose a significant investment sum that causes you to freak out, you can bet you're going to make some bad decisions in the future. Likewise, there are going to be times when you win big money, and it's easy to get excited and want to invest more and make more. This is called greed and can backfire just as badly.

Being a day trader means being able to stand calm and relaxed in even the most stressful of situations, removing emotion from your decision-making process, sticking to your plan, and remaining grounded. If you're not this sort of person, or you can't cultivate this kind of mindset, then day trading is probably not for you.

Setting Up Your Finances

Being able to manage your finances is vital before you set into the world of day trading. If you have any kind of debt right now, you shouldn't even consider day trading until you've cleared it. If you have a loan or credit card, or both, where you're paying back interest rates of 20%, and you're only making a 5% return on your investments, then you're going to be losing money.

Instead, make sure you're paying off all your debts and then getting your capital ready. This way, you'll be minimizing how much interest you're paying on your credit and debt and then maximizing your profits when you start investing.

Once you're in the green, you need to start thinking about getting your capital in place. This is the starting amount of money you're going to be investing with. This can vary dramatically depending on your personal situation, so it's really up to you. You could start small, perhaps with $5,000 and then day trade part-time. As your capital grows over time, you can then begin transitioning over to becoming a full-time trader.

On the other hand, you may want to save up a lump sum that means you can quit your job and start investing straight away, although that's not recommended since you'll have no experience. Even if you have a lump sum, start small, so you can teach yourself the ropes of trading, and then start investing more and more once you start gathering experience.

Van Tharp, one of the top day traders in the world and author of Trade Your Way to Financial Freedom, recommends that if you're trading full-time, you're going to want around $100,000 to start with. If you're looking to day trade effectively, you're going to want approximately $10,000 in your trading account at all times.

The final financial aspect you'll want to consider is getting yourself a rainy-day emergency fund. This means creating a savings account where you put a recommended three months' worth of living expenses into an account and then leave it.

This means when you're trading, and if you ever come across a time in your life where you're suffering from financial difficulties, you'll have this fund to fall back on. However, you need to remember this is not an account you can ever use for trading or investment. If you have a hard-losing streak and you need money to live on to support yourself and your family, you don't want to end up with nothing. This is a financial crisis you'll want to avoid at all costs, which is why it's best to be as prepared as possible.

Learn About Stock Market Trading

This should go without saying, but if you want to become a day trader, you need to have some kind of passion or interest in the stock market world, or at least the drive to become educated about it. You need to learn when the stock market trading hours are and how the processes and systems within the stock market work.

You should have an interest in a particular niche or industry you want to trade in, and you better have some kind of passion surrounding it because you're going to need to be watching the news on this industry, reading articles and books on the subjects, and investing your time watching interviews and learning about these stock market companies in terms of how they work and what they're up too on a daily basis.

You'll also need to learn about what stocks actually, as well as other potential trading options, such as ETFs, options, futures, and mutual funds. We'll briefly describe each one in the table below, but it's crucial you take time to develop a clear understanding of each other before you start implementing a trading strategy and investing in one.

Stocks When the ownership of a company or organization is broken down into all the shares, these are individually known as "stocks." Each stock represents a fractional ownership of a company relative to the number of shares it has in total.

ETFs The term shortened for 'Exchanged-Traded Funds,' ETFs are a type of investment fund that is traded identically to a stock on the stock market and exchanges of the world. ETFs are indexes made of other securities and assets, such as stocks, special funds, and commodity funds.

Options is the term given to a contract that gives a specific buyer a right to buy or sell any underlying asset, although it doesn't guarantee an obligation for sale. However, options will give the price that must be valid prior to or on a specified date stated on the option contract.

Futures are another type of contract that points to the legal agreement that contracts the buying and selling of something at a price, time, and date that has been predetermined. However, these metrics won't be known by the parties involved and is classed as an asset.

Mutual Funds Mutual funds are investment portfolios that are managed by professional financial services. These services bring in money from several investors to buy stocks, shares, and other securities, like the ones in this table.

Gold & Precious Metals Gold (and sometimes other precious metals) refers to the trading asset of the metal gold that is stored in banks around the US and around the world.

Eminis are another type of futures contracts that track the S&P 500 stock index market. It is also known as the E-Mini, ES, or just Mini.

Cryptocurrencies this is a broad term that refers to the trade of cryptocurrencies within the stock market. This can be done individually or via an exchange.

Forex is the trading of foreign currencies around the world by converting one currency into another and then continuing to trade in this manner.

Practice Your Money Management Skills

The last thing you need to do before you even start to think about getting ready to trade stocks is to consider how effective your money management skills are. If you're thinking to yourself, 'yeah, my money management skills are pretty good,' then take a step back and consider how you can improve. There's always room to be better, and as a day trader, these are improvements you're going to both want and need.

Consider this. If you're starting with $100,000 and you're using a tried-and-tested strategy that has a 60% success rate, how much are you going to invest to begin with? What happens if your first four trades fail and come out as a loss? How should you be allocating your capital?

With any kind of trading, it's always a good idea to start small and then expand over time. It's rather stupid to jump in on your first trade and buy $100,000 worth of stock and just hope for the best. Of course, it might pay off, but if you're this risky with your first investment, the chances are it's going to backfire dramatically later down the line.

Work on your money management skills and nurture the ability to step back and make decisions from a grounded state of mind. You need to be able to wisely select which opportunities you're going to invest in and how you're going to manage your investment capital. Even if you're using a strategy that has a 30% success rate, you can still make a large amount of profit from it when you have proper money management skills.

Once you've developed all these aspects of your life and you've got yourself ready, you're one step closer to starting your day trading career. Before we really jump into the meat of what you need to do and actually start investing, there's one more aspect we need to cover, and that's developing your day trading mindset.

Why Do You Trade?

Answer: It's simple—the only reason to trade is to make money! This question, why do you trade, is important and something to think about as we conclude this topic.

While the answer "to make money" might seem obvious—a no-brainer—most losing traders actually trade for other reasons. They may think they are trading to make money, but their actions indicate that other motivations are driving their decisions. Remember, the most important indicator is you.

If you are truly trading to make money, then the next logical question to ask is how... How does a trader achieve that objective?

The answer is by trading within the context and rules of a proven trade plan. A proven trade plan grows equity in your account, despite the random distribution of wins and losses. It includes rules to follow that you can prove to yourself.

Taking random trades that are not within the context of a proven trade plan is not trading to make money. It is something else. Why? Because we are traders. It is what we do. We take trades. If you win on a random trade, now what? There is still another trade to take, right? Making money comes from the edge that your proven trade plan gives you over time. Random trades are not going to reveal whether or not you have an edge—they're random—until after the fact, when you will most likely learn that the answer is no, you did not have an edge. And then it will be too late. This is how accounts get blown up.

If you are truly trading to make money, then your actions should reflect that. If they do not, then you are most likely trading for other reasons that you don't quite understand. You will need to address that if you truly want to internalize the correct reason to trade—to make money. Otherwise, the market will give you something else, and you probably will not like it.

CHAPTER 4:

Risk and Account Management

Since the goal of every good trader is to make a profit, to be a good and successful one, you have to learn how to manage risks related to your trading and how to protect your profits. How well you manage your risks determines how successful you will be as a trader.

Prepare your mind because you are about to learn straightforward but powerful and practical techniques in risk management strategies and techniques.

Planning Your Trade

A Chinese military general, Sun Tzu, once said: "Every battle is won before it is fought," this implies that planning and strategy are essential in trading. Planning is inevitable. It is just like the famous quote says, "Plan the trade and trade the plan." This determines the success or failure of your trade; no successful trader goes into the deal without carefully planning out the trade, pointing out possible future losses, calculating risks, and listing out potential future profits in your trade.

A plan should be written down clearly and concisely; your plan can change with changes in the market; risk tolerance should also be incorporated. Here are some steps you must follow for a successful trade plan:

Skill Assessment: here, you should be able to assess yourself very well to determine how ready you are to trade. You should ask yourself a very crucial question such as: are you prepared to trade? How much confidence do you have in a particular market? Have you tested your system by paper trading? (Paper trading is a way of practicing buying and selling without investing real money, it is usually done using online trading platforms such as paper Money and Investopedia) How sure are you that your system will work in a live trading environment? Can you spot and follow your signals without delaying?

Mental preparation: As a good trader, you should be emotionally and mentally prepared for the upcoming tasks, you should be prepared for whatever situation that might arise and whatever changes that may occur in your market. Avoid distractions as much as possible in your trading area.

If you are emotionally incapable, try taking a day off, take some rest, do some exercise. This keeps your brain ready for the upcoming task because trading has a lot of thinking associated with it.

Also, have a market mantra before the day begins; it is a kind of special quote or phrase that gets you ready for trading.

Set Risk Level: this determines how much of your portfolio you should risk on a trade. Your portfolio includes all financial assets, such as bonds, stocks, and currencies, cash, commodities, and cash equivalents. This depends on how you choose to trade and the risks tolerance; It can vary, but it should be within the range of 1% to 5% of your portfolio on a given trading day. If you lose any of that amount of money in a day, leave that market immediately and save your portfolio for a better market.

Consider the One-Percent Rule

Most successful traders make use of what is called the one-percent rule; it merely states that you should never invest more than 1% of your capital or portfolio into a single trade or market. This means that if you have $10,000 in your trading account, the highest amount you would invest should not be above $100 per single trade.

This technique is usually done by traders with accounts with less than $100,000. Some other traders may decide to go as high as 2%. It all depends on your position and the size of your account. The best thing to do is to keep the rule at least below 2%.

Setting Stop-Loss and Profit Points

Just like the name implies, a stop-loss point occurs when a trader decides to sell a stock and bear the loss, this situation usually happens when the market doesn't turn out well enough for the trader. The stock's in the market goes way below expected, hence before the stock's value could get any lower, the trader decides to sell it out. The take profit point is the price at which a trader will sell a stock and gain a profit from the trade. Traders usually sell before a period of consolidation takes place.

How to More Effectively Set Stop-Loss Points

Setting stop-loss points in order to have profit is usually made in technical analysis, although fundamental analysis can help out. A great way of setting stop-loss or take profit levels is by resistance trend lines; this can be done by connecting and comparing past highs or lows.

Diversify and Hedge

To diversify and the hedge is just like the famous phrase, "never put all your eggs in one basket." If you choose to put all your money in one stock, you are taking a significant risk. So spread your investments across different sectors. There may also be times when you need to hedge at a particular position considering stock and the market.

The Bottom Line

As a good trader, you should be able to know when to enter or leave a trade. By using the stop-loss, the trader can minimize losses. It is better to plan ahead of time.

Calculating Expected Return

Calculating expected returns is very crucial in managing risks, it helps you think through your trade, and it is a perfect way to compare trades in order to choose the most profitable and less risky ones. Returns can be calculated thus:

[(Probability of gain) × (take profit % gain)] + [(probability of loss) × (stop-loss % loss)]

The end of this should give the expected returns.

Day Trading Risks

To become a successful trader, you need to aware of the various risks that you are bound to face before getting into the trading world. There are three major categories of risks:

Market Risks

Understanding market changes in your trade is an essential aspect of your business. Understanding when the markets rise and fall, coupled with the possible risks associated with it, will help you to protect your profit more. Types of market risks include:

Inflation risk: inflation occurs when there is uncertainty in the future value of an investment you are making. While deflation may mean more returns and profit for you. Rising inflation often reduces the returns and profit you'd be expecting from it. This also means that as prices of stocks and commodities increases, the demand for it decreases. Hence, you should prepare your plan for any market changes at all.

Marketability risk: this tells how sellable your investment is. If there is any form of resistance or delay in selling or marketing your investment effectively, then your target market won't mean anything. For example, if you choose to invest in a small company whose stock isn't sold on one of the major stock markets, then you risk losing your investment for nothing.

Currency translation risk: this usually occurs when you are trading with foreign countries when there are fluctuations between the values of your local currency and the currency of your international trading country. A piece of useful knowledge about currency trading risk would be very beneficial to traders because even if your stock or investment rises in price, you can still lose money depending on the currency exchange rate between the two countries. If the value of your local currency falls against the other currency, your investment can be far smaller when you convert it back.

Investment Risks

This suggests how you invest your money and manage how you enter into or leave trades. There are two major kinds of risks:

Opportunity risks: this kind of investment risk shuts or stops you from investing in other more profitable trades due to the fact that your money is already tied up in your current business. This type of risk makes you lose golden opportunities, all because your money is blocked by another one.

Concentration risks: this happens when you focus all your investment and capital in just one particular trade, perhaps because you think that you have found your dream trade that will make you a millionaire. Hence you invest all you've got, leaving yourself very vulnerable to any potential risks that might arise in that trade with the possibility of losing it all.

Trading Risks

Trading risks are common risks that swing traders usually encounter, and every trader needs to know about them, just as the saying "knowledge is power," you need to be knowledgeable about them, and this will give you leverage in managing the future risks that may arise. Some common risks that are associated with trading risks include:

Slippage risk: this risk gives attention to some hidden costs that may be related to every transaction the trader makes. Every time you enter or leave a trade, there is some very minor and little subtraction of money from your account. Also, every time you buy a stock at the asking price, which is the lowest price available for the stock that you want, and sells it at the bid price, which is the highest price someone is willing to pay for your shares, you have to know that it is always less than the asking price. At first, the amount for each trade may seem small, but as your trading increases, the amounts you also lose gains.

Poor execution risk: this risk occurs when your broker has a difficult time filling out your order, perhaps due to fast market conditions, inadequate availability of stock, and the absence of other buyers and sellers. When this happens, you risk having your stock trade going below than it should or not getting your order filled at all.

Gap risk: this occurs when there are price gaps in your transactions; sometimes, a stock opens at a significantly high or lesser price and sometimes may trade using your exit price. For example, a stock may close at $35 today and begin at $30 tomorrow. If your planned price is $34, your order is likely to be filled out at the opening price. Though these kinds of risks are infrequent, they can cause problems for most traders.

Other Types of Risks Include

BLACK SWAN EVENTS: these are the type of risks that comes up unexpectedly. They are tough to predict. It is a type of significant risk that has a substantial impact on the market.

UNDIVERSIFIED RISK: this is a type of risk that occurs when you 'put all your eggs in one basket.' This type of risk is usually tough to avoid and difficult to predict as markets can also influence this type of risk. This type is one of the primary reasons why investors and traders usually decide to diversify their stocks and money, avoiding the risk of losing everything at once.

CHAPTER 5:

Psychology Discipline

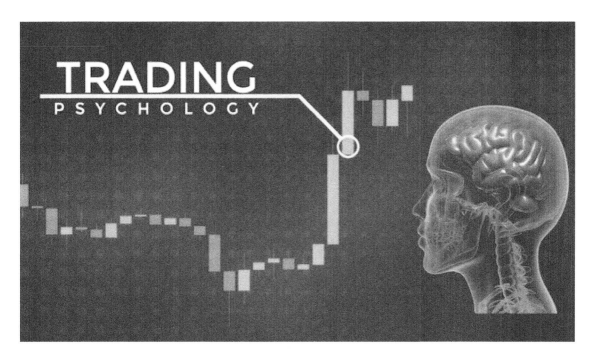

Trading with Emotions

It is common for traders to have their emotions and feelings jumbled up when day trading, from the highs and the lows they experience from the market. This is a far outcry from the confident self that a trader usually poses before the markets open, bubbling up with excitement over the money and profits that they intend to make. Emotions in trading can mess up and impair your judgment and your ability to make wise decisions. Day trading is not to be carried out without emotions, but rather as a trader. You should know how to work your way around them, making them work for your good. A clear level headed and stable mind should be kept at all times, whether your profits are on the rise or whether you are on a losing streak. This is not to mean that as a trader, you are to disconnect from your emotions.

Greed

A trader may be fueled to earn more money by checking their balances in their accounts and seeing it be as of a low level. While this may be a motivator to work hard, some traders take it too far, wanting to earn a lot of money right there and then. They make mistakes while trading that has reverse effects than the intended ones...

Taking Unnecessary Risks

Greed for more money will seek to convince the trader to take risks that are not worth so as to achieve a certain financial threshold in the trading account. These will most likely end up in losses. The risky traders may take risks such as high leverage that they hope will work in their favor, but at the same time may have them making huge losses.

Making an Overtrade

Due to the urge to make more and more money, a trader may extend over long periods of time trading. Commonly these efforts are in vain, for overtrading through the highs and the lows of the market put a trader in a position where their accounts can be wiped off as a result of greed. Not putting into account the time of trading and plunging into opening up trades without having done an analysis will most likely result in a loss.

Improper Profit and Loss Comprehension

Wanting to earn a lot of money within a short period of time will have a trader not closing a trade that is losing, maintaining the losses, and on the other hand, overriding on profit-making trade until a reverse in the market happens, canceling out all the gains made.

Fear

Fear can work in both directions, as a limit to an over-trade or also as a limit to making profits. A trader may close a trade so as to avert a loss, the action motivated by fear. A trader may also close a trade too early, even when on a winning streak in making gains, in fear that the market will reverse and that there will be losses. In both scenarios, fear is the motivator, working in avoiding failure and success at the same time.

The Fear to Fail

The fear of failing in trading may inhibit a trader from opening up trades and just watch as the market changes and goes in cycles when doing nothing. The fear of failing in trading is an inhibitor to success. It prevents a trader from executing what could have been a successful trade.

The Fear to Succeed

This type of fear in trading psychology will make a trader lose out his profits to the market when there was an opportunity to do otherwise. It works in a self-harming way in the market scenarios. Such traders in this category fear having too much profit and allow losses to run, all while aware of their activities and the losses they are going to make.

Bias in Trading

There are several market biases that a trader may tend to make that may be a result of emotional play, which traders are advised against. In the psychology of trading, these biases may influence a trader to make unwise and uncalculated trading decisions that may prove to be loss-making ones. Even when the trading biases are in focus, as a trader, you have to be aware of the emotions in you and come up with ways to keep them in check and maintain a cool head in your trading window.

Bias in Overconfidence

It is a common occurrence with traders, especially new traders, that when you make a trade with huge profits, you get in euphoria in the state of winning. You want to go on opening up trades with the belief that your analysis cannot go wrong, boiling down to the profits and gains you've made.

This should not be the case. One cannot be too overexcited and overconfident in the analysis skills that you believe you cannot make a loss. The market is a volatile one, and therefore the cards can change at any given time, and when they do, the over-excited and overconfident trader now turns into a disappointing one.

Bias in Confirming Trades

In trading psychology, the bias in confirmation of a trade you have already made, justifying it, is one of the factors that waste a lot of time and money for traders. This type of bias is mostly associated with professional traders. After making a trade, they go back to evaluate and analyze the trade they just made, trying to prove that it was the correct one, whether they sailed according to the market.

They waste a lot of time digging for information that they are already aware of. They could also be proving that the mistake they made in opening a wrong trade and making a wrong move was a correct one.

Bias in Anchoring on Obsolete Strategies

This type of bias in the psychology of trading applies to the traders that rely so much on outdated information and obsolete strategies that do more harm than good to their trading success.

Anchoring on the correct but irrelevant information when trading might make the trader susceptible to making losses, a blow to the traders who are always lazy to dig up for new information on the market. Keeping up with the current events and factors that may have an impact on the market is one of the key aspects of having a successful trading career.

Bias in Avoiding Losses

Trading with the motive to avert losses usually boils down to the fear factor. There are some traders whose trading patterns and their trading windows are controlled by fear of making losses. Having gains and making profits is not a motivation to them when fear hinders them from opening trades that could have otherwise been profitable. They also close trades too early, even when making profits in a bid to avert the losses, their imaginable losses.

Psychology Affecting Traders' Habits

Psychological aspects affect habits in trading, the mistakes, and the winning strategies that a trader comes up with. Explained below are the negative habits that many traders make with the influence of psychology on their habits.

Trading Without a Strategy

With no trading strategy and plan, a trader will face challenges with no place to refer to the anticipated end result. A proper strategy should be drawn by a trader to be a referencing point when facing a problem in trading in the market. It should be a clearly constructed plan, detailing what to do in certain situations and which type of trading patterns to employ in different case scenarios. Trading without a strategy is akin to trading to lose your money.

Lack of Money Management Plans

Money management plans are one of the main aspects of trading, and without solid strategies in this, it is difficult to make progress in making gains in the trades opened. As a trader, you have to abide by certain principles that will guide you in how to spend your money in the account in opening up trades and ensuring that profits ensue from that.

Wanting to Be Always Right

Some traders always go against the market, placing their desire of what manner they would like the market to behave in. They do not follow the sign that the market points to, but rather they follow their own philosophy, not doing proper analysis and always wanting to be right.

Remedying the Effects of Psychological Habits

Coming Up with Clear Cut Goals

Drawing clear and concise goals and strategies to trade helps a trader in having a vision of trading and just not doing it for the sake of trading. Writing down goals also works to improve the confidence levels of the trader. Working with a well comprehensive strategy is a profit-making plan in the market.

Setting Up Rules for Trading

Rules for the trader work for the good in ensuring discipline in trading. As a trader, you should come up with rules that govern the time of the day that you start trading, the time that you close your trades, and whether or not you trade on a daily basis, or whatever your trading window is. Rules are the backbone of successful trading; when to close a losing trade and at the same time when to close a winning one.

Initializing Money Management Strategies

Coming up with money strategies is not enough, but also actualizing the strategies is equally important.

Money management strategies are of great importance in ensuring that a trader's profitability is put first, putting into consideration the risk of loss. Put the money strategy into action to avoid trading haphazardly and trading with emotions.

CHAPTER 6:

Build Your Watch List

A Trading Watch List

As an active day trader, you must create a trading watch list. Basically, this is a list where you record the daily share prices of a group of stocks over time. It acts like a menu for the trading day. Based on the fundamental and technical new catalyst, a trading watch list should have active stocks that are ready to trade. It can either be done on the notepad, a spreadsheet, or even on paper. There are many software programs and other utilities that help in generating a watch list. It can also be provided by some brokerage houses where you pay a minimal charge, or for free.

A trader can have more than one watch list, but there are two specific watch lists that every active trader should never mess; a general watch list and a dynamic watch list. The general one may be composed of hundreds of stocks that are familiar to the trader. Every trader should also narrow down from the general watch list and come up with an active stock watch list every trading day before the market opening. This watch list should have stocks that the trader has been watching for days or weeks that may be about to set up for a technical movement. Unlike the general list, the active trade list should not contain too many stocks. It should have a handful of ripe stocks that the trader is comfortable to trade. In other words, a general watch list may contain shares that the trader has already purchased recently or in the past, while the active watch list should contain stocks that the trader is considering to purchase. For example, let's say that you are an active trader with ten positions on average at any given time. Usually, you will be tracking several stocks so that you can purchase another position from the watch list immediately after one position has been sold. This will help you avoid a situation where at any given time you have a lot of idle cash in your trading account. A watch list is convenient for many different reasons. For example, let's say that you have done your research and found a company that you feel is sound and has promising potential, but the stock value seems to be currently high or overvalued. You decide to wait for a better convenient time so that you can buy. You will use the watch list to track the stock price and generate charts to monitor the stock trends. That way, you will be able to know the best time to purchase that stock.

Building Your Trading Watch List

Stocks in Play

When a stock is widely believed to be a takeover target, it is said to be in play. Day traders widely trade stocks in play because their volatility produces reasonable risks and trading opportunities. When company stocks have less volatility, they move slowly, and they only have a reasonable price change only when the company shows good or bad trading outcomes. This may occur only a few times in a year. Such companies are ideal for investors looking for returns in the long-term. Long term investors buy shares in these companies, which have good prospects, with shares moving slowly in the right direction, and it matters less to them if the share price doesn't move much intraday. But day traders buy and sell stocks during stock market opening hours and exit the trade before the day ends. Sometimes they even trade for a few minutes or an hour and exit the market. They, therefore, require more action than investors. They need stocks that move and produce price swings so that their trade becomes worthwhile. Such fluctuations in prices leave enough room for them to realize profits after paying the association fees charged by stockbrokers for buying and selling shares.

Stocks in play also have a large volume. Day traders are after quick entries and exits, and they want liquid stocks. That means they can buy and sell shares in the stock on demand. A stock that doesn't have good liquidity and my cost the broker time to strike a promising buying or selling deal. The broker is unable to negotiate the deal that the trader wants to buy or sell at. For day traders, this is a problem because it means the difference between a profitable trade and a non-profitable one. Day traders are guided by trade volumes of shares that are traded each day to arrive at what they consider good liquidity for them. For most traders, one hundred thousand shares traded per day would be their minimum, while some other traders may require a million shares.

Stocks in play will change in one day. An ordinary stock will be put in play by the company news, which is typically released early in the morning, and it will vary depending on the nature of the new, whether it is good or bad.

Sometimes good news for traders may be bad news for investors. Some of the big companies like Apple, Amazon, and Facebook have stocks that are always in play, and day traders will have these stocks constantly on their watch list. This is because they have large volumes of trades and traded shares. This is where a day trader looks for excellent trading opportunities and proper levels to trade from.

Other websites have free stock screening tools that help traders to find stocks that are in rapid movement, intraday, and break out pre-market. These are websites like Market watch and busy stock. Breakout shares and top lists for trending UK shares are produced by ADVFN. They also have apps like Seeking Alpha, with live news feeds that are accessible for you. Big company news and breaking news are quickly reported by news channels like CNN, BBC, Reuters, and Bloomberg. Up to the minute, relevant news for day traders is also provided by channels like Stock twits.

Float and Market Cap

As an active day trader, it is crucial to understand the link between company size, risk, and return potential. Such information is vital as you lay the foundation to pursue long-term trading goals. With such knowledge, you can build a balanced watch list that comprises different market caps.

Market cap means market capitalization. It expresses the stock value of all the company shares. To arrive at the market cap of an entity, multiply the entities' shares by the stock price.

An Entity with $50 million in shares with each share trading at $20, then $10 billion will be its market cap. Market cap is necessary because it helps traders to understand and compare the size of different companies. Market cap helps you to know the worth of different companies in the open market. It also helps you to understand how the market perceives a particular company and mirrors what investors and traders are ready to pay for its stock.

Large-cap stocks: $10 billion and over is their stock market value. Typically, these are reputable companies that produce quality goods and services. They experience steady growth and have a history of consistency in dividend payments to their shareholders. Their brand names are familiar to national and even international consumer audience. They are dominant players in their respective industries of the establishment. They are ideal for conservative investors since they pose less risk as they have less growth potential.

Mid-cap stocks: Typically, these are businesses with a minimum market value of $2billion and a maximum market value of 10$billion. In other words, their market value is between $2billion and $10 billion. They are medium-sized, established companies with growth potential. Such companies are experiencing rapid growth, or there is an expectation that they will grow rapidly in the near future. They are in the stage of boosting their competitive advantage and widening their share of the market. This is a crucial stage since it determines their ability to attain maximum potential. In terms of risk, they have less risk in comparison with new startups.

When it comes to potential, they offer more potential than blue-chip companies since they are expected to continue to grow until they reach full potential.

Small caps: their market stock value ranges from $300 million to $2 billion. They are growing businesses that are just emerging in the industry. They are the riskiest and the most aggressive and rely on niche marketing to survive in the industry. Due to limited resources, they are vulnerable to economic shocks. They are susceptible to intense competition and market uncertainties. Since they are new startups, they have high growth potential in the long-term, and they are ideal for investors who can cope up with volatile stock price swings in the short-run.

Float, on the other hand, is the number of shares, which are available for trading by the general public. Unlike the market cap that calculates the total stock value of all company shares, free-float does not include locked-in shares. Locked-in shares are those that are held by company employees and the government. Market cap can be affected by several factors. When there is a significant change in the value of shares, either up or down, this can have an impact on the market cap. Market cap can also be impacted when the number of issued shares changes. Market cap can be diluted when warrants are exercised on the stock of the company because the number of shares outstanding will increase. This is because such an exercise is often carried out below the shares market price, hence it has the potential to impact on the market cap. On the other hand, issuing a dividend or a stock split typically doesn't alter the market cap.

To build a stable watch list, comprising large-cap, mid-cap, and small-cap stocks, a trader will have to evaluate their time horizon, risk tolerance, and financial goals. A balanced watch list comprising all the market caps may be ideal in helping to reduce the investment risk.

Pre-Market Gappers

Pre-market trading refers to trading activities that take place between 8 am, and 9:30 am EST every trading day. This is usually before the regular market session begins. Traders and investors monitor the pre-market trading period to judge the direction and the strength of the market while waiting for the regular trading session. During the pre-market activity, there is limited liquidity and volume. Wide bid-ask spreads are a common thing during the pre-market period. The type of orders that can be used during this period is limited by many retail brokers, even though they offer pre-market trading. As early as 4 am, direct-access brokers begin to allow access to the pre-market activity to start. It is crucial to bear in mind that there is limited activity during this pre-market period.

The most reliable types of stocks that are beneficial to trade during pre-market activities are gapper or dumper. They are usually viable during the seasons when earnings for various companies are reported. During such season, these stocks gap with the volume either up or down. They are usually triggered by a primary catalyst such as press releases, news, or earnings reports. They can also be reacting to rumors or analyst upgrades or downgrades. It is important to note that stocks tend to get more 'tradability,' follow-through, and consistent volume when they are gapped in reaction to earnings reports and guidance. As you trade during pre-market activity, you should always know that this period is characterized by fewer participants, wider spread, and thin liquidity. It is not advisable to trade pre-market unless there is a substantial volume gap that is being driven by a catalyst. Waiting for the market to open is the most suitable option for most traders.

CHAPTER 7:

Why Most Day Traders Lose

With the numerous benefits that can be gained from day trading, it begs to question why most day traders fail. If the activity is as lucrative as it sounds, why do most of these traders fail? Understanding why traders fail gives you some insight into the common mistakes that traders fail, which makes them lose money. Accordingly, you will be better placed to trade wisely by avoiding common pitfalls in such trading. Here is a look at some of the reasons why traders fail.

Relying On Random

Let's assume we have a new trader in the market called John. John has some knowledge about the market just because he always watches the news more so on stock markets. However, John has never traded. Since he has some basic market knowledge, he feels that he can try out day trading. To this point, John has never sat down to write down some strategies which he could implement to trade on stocks. So, he opens up an account and purchases 400 shares without thinking.

Fortunately, to his advantage, the stocks rise during his lunch hour period. After lunch, John decides to sell off his shares. His first sale earns him a $100 profit. His second attempt also earns him $100. Now, John has the feeling that indeed he is a good trader. In just a day, he has managed to earn $200.

After a careful analysis of John's situation, an experienced trader would argue that John's day trading activity could easily be short-lived. In John's example, he faces the risk of losing money if he gains the perception that his strategies are working. Interestingly, he might be tempted to increase his shares because he knows that he will earn a profit. It is important to understand that John's strategies are untested. Therefore, there is no guarantee that his trading activity could earn him returns over the long-run.

The danger that John faces here is that he believes in his formulated and untested strategies. Consequently, he might overlook recommended trading techniques that would have helped him avoid common mistakes. In the end, when he loses money, he will be disappointed arguing that day trading is not lucrative. This is the trap that most newbies enter into. Their first luck in online trading blinds them from realizing the need for constant learning in this activity.

Abandoning Strategy

Assuming that John learned his mistakes and corrected them in his future trades. Now, he relies on a strategy that helps him find success in day trading for about a year or two. At this point, John feels that he has found the right strategy that works for him. However, there is another problem that ensues. John realizes that his plan has led him to losses for more than six times now. He is in a huge dilemma, wondering what to do since he cannot continue making losses.

So, what does John do; he decides to adopt another strategy. Regardless of the success that he enjoyed using his previous plan, John now feels that it is time to switch to another strategy. Ideally, this is a new and untested strategy that he will be adopting. One thing that you should realize here is that John is going for a strategy that is not tested. He is abandoning a strategy that has worked for about two years now. The risk here is that John could find himself where he started. He could incur losses because of his abandoning strategy.

Here, you should learn that randomness can lead to profits and that it can also drive a trader to incur losses. To ensure that such randomness is avoided, it is recommended for a trader to have a solid plan that they stick to. This is a plan that will define how they trade. A good plan ought to lay their entry and exit strategies. Also, the plan should stipulate the money management technique, which will help a trader use their money wisely.

Lack of Knowledge

A major reason why most traders fail is their lack of market knowledge. By failing to educate themselves about stock markets, they find themselves in a ditch. You cannot count yourself as a trader just because you buy and sell shares. Certainly not! You have to learn how to analyze the securities which you will be buying. Your broker might not give you all the information that you need to become a good trader. So, don't assume that reading magazines and newspapers will get you the market info that you need. A prudent trader knows the significance of working with a profitable trading plan. They understand why it is imperative for them to analyze stocks effectively to determine whether they are buying profitable stocks or not. More importantly, a wise trader should know of ideal strategies that they will employ to manage their finances shrewdly. Don't believe day trading myths circulating over the internet. Do your homework by researching and educating yourself about stock markets.

Unfitting Mindset

We are human beings with emotions. However, being overly emotional can be dangerous in an uncertain trading environment. To become a successful trader, you need to work on your emotions. The topic of trading psychology, which will be later discussed, will educate you on the importance of developing the right mindset in online trading. Dealing with your emotions will have a huge impact on whether you close your day with losses or profits. Hence, it is very important that you keep your emotions in check.

Rigidity to Market Changes

One thing that you can be sure of is that trading markets will always change. There is no guarantee that a particular market will rise steadily throughout the buying and selling period. If this were the case, then everybody would have been traders. The best traders will always adjust to market changes. They will know when to buy and when to sell. Before jumping to purchase a particular stock, it is advisable to conduct scenario analysis. Afterward, you should devise strategic moves that will ensure that you make profits while lowering the chances of incurring losses.

Learning from Mistakes

You often hear people say that failing is part of succeeding. Well, this is true. Unfortunately, it stands as one of the main reasons why day traders fail. Learning by making mistakes here and there will cost a day trader a lot of money. Engaging in trial and error is what discourages most traders from any attempt to put their money in stocks. Some even end up arguing that day trading is a form of gambling. To circumvent this problem, one should learn from other experienced traders. This way, you will reduce the chances of making losses. Equally, you will learn the tricks which can be utilized to take advantage of market volatility. Therefore, do not choose to learn how to trade through trial and error. You will only lose a lot of money beyond your expectations.

Unrealistic Expectations

Take a breather! Indeed, day trading is a profitable activity that can earn you a living. Nonetheless, this should not blind you from realizing that losses can also be made. You cannot get rich overnight with day trading. However, it is a slow and gradual process that will see your money multiply. Traders fail because they try to force returns to cover for the huge losses that they have made. Having the right plan and sticking to it will help you in toning down your expectations. Deep inside, you should have it in mind that you are trading for a living. Therefore, patience is important.

Poor Money Management

The effort that you put into finding a working strategy is the same effort that you should put in managing your finances. A trader should stick to a plan that defines the amount of money that they will risk on a regular basis. The money risked should give the trader the satisfaction that it is worth the rewards they anticipate. Having enough funds set aside for the trading activity should not give one the impression that they need to splash their money on stocks. As a matter of fact, the more you have as capital, the more you should preserve.

The bottom line is that traders can deal with their possibilities of failing by sticking to a plan. Sticking to a trading plan will mean that you are disciplined enough to know the exact amount of money you will risk. It also implies that you will employ a buying and selling strategy that works for you. Most importantly, you will also give yourself time to learn what there is to learn about day trading.

CHAPTER 8:

Characteristics of Winning Traders

Anyone can indeed become a day trader, but to survive in the highly competitive market in the long run, you need to adapt yourself according to this business's requirement. You need to develop some qualities that will differentiate you from others and help you sustain as a day trader. Let's look at some of those characteristics of successful traders:

They Take Full Responsibility

Good traders accept their losses, and they do not dwell on or blame others or conditions. They learn from their failures and carry on their trade. There is a system for successful traders.

They adhere to their system of trade religiously. Many established traders are willing to take responsibility for their success; few are willing to take responsibility for failure.

There is no talk of the market-maker or broker somehow when they win, the market behaving strangely, the system, their risk management, or mind-affecting their trade. However, these bugaboos, all of a sudden, appear at the frontline of their thinking during a loss. There is a tendency, when things do not go your way, to look at someone other than yourself, the one who pushed the buttons. Having a responsibility to the gut-level does not distinguish winners from losers. They are identical. In the situation, they all came from the common denominator - you. Will you build up your ego when you excel, or do you draw on what you have done right to do more? Trading holds a mirror to oneself, sees what needs work, and works on it while seeing what works and increasing it. And it is your weakest trading skill that sets the height of your earnings and success. Fortunately, skill is a drill that can easily be molded to build your success's pillars.

They Have a Lot of Patience

Successful traders know most of the positions the minute that they are opened. They have to wait for their moment to come. They are patient enough to handle all the trading uncertainty. Most traders come up with a strategy that helps them decide when and where to enter a trade. That strategy should yield a profit if it is traded correctly. It sounds easy, but traders are facing a problem:

when they see a fast-moving chart in real, their mind gets fooled into thinking that you enter a trade before the market structure is fully developed. You are afraid to lose out on a trade, so you enter early and usually end up losing.

Wait for the right setup and trigger your trade ultimately. You also need to be ok with missing an opportunity; take only trades that will give you the right setup and trigger your trade. There should be no trades unless the market causes this.

Have a brainstorming session about what you could do better if you are following your plan and still get into it a bit too early. If the price is higher and begins to go down, consider waiting for that to happen before considering getting in. When the price starts moving sideways, look for small clues that the price is beginning to rise again. If the movement lasts, waiting for the price to go high to cause the trade can help. If the price wiggles around during that pullback, consider watching those tiny price shifts inside the pullback for higher highs and higher lows.

These movements prove the buying pressure will build up again. When the price appears to shift opposite right before it moves in the direction you are expecting, you are waiting for the move to take place and then act. Do not trade until you are sure now is the time to get in. You do not have to capture every big move in prices to make a profit. When you miss a step, then you are missing it.

Be patient; the market takes longer than we would expect to move. By waiting for the right setup and trigger, you will begin to catch more of the price movements you anticipate and not waste your money on losing trades.

They Have Forward Thinking

Successful day traders cannot get trapped in the past. Although day traders are using past data to help them make trading decisions, they must be able to apply the information in real-time. Traders are also plotting their next moves, deciding what they will do depending on where the market is going.

The markets are not static. We cannot decide in five minutes we are going to buy at a certain amount and then forget all the market knowledge that is going on in those five minutes. Day traders are preparing their next move always, based on new market information they receive every second. They consider various scenarios that might be carried out and then prepare how they would execute their trading strategy for each of those different conditions.

They Do Not Overtrade

Overtrading is the unnecessary buying or selling of financial instruments. In many terms, getting too many open positions on a single trade or using a disproportionate amount of capital. There are no laws or regulations for individual traders against overtrading, but this can damage your portfolio. Overtrading can have significant implications for trading brokers, as they are controlled bodies. It is best to avoid overtrading and have a comprehensive trading plan and risk management strategy in place. Stop emotional trading: differentiate between logical and emotional trading decisions and provide sound reasoning for your decisions.

When you already have more than one open position, by spreading your investment through asset groups, you can help reduce risk. Using just what you have: determine how much you want to gamble but never use more money to trade than you can afford to lose. Good traders should not overtrade. They know that overtrading put their account at risk, and not everybody knows it is the day of the trade. They are waiting for an opponent with high probability.

They Are Adaptable

Successful traders are capable of adapting. They customize their trading methods and market-changing decisions. Successful traders understand what kind of dealer they are.

They do not force themselves to trade in methods or strategies; their personality does not fit. You are permitted to make small adjustments to your trading plan after a full month of trading, based on what you learned from your trading plan review sessions. Trades focused on these minor strategic improvements should be exercised for another month and evaluated afterward. Changes should not be made to the plan before the one month, because it is easy to make changes based on individual trades as opposed to overall results.

The issues that come up in your self-review are being worked on every day. For the self-review, all you have to do is follow the trading strategy, whatever it might be. If the trading strategy evolves, so does your company, but it is always your job to follow the strategy. Your daily self-examination does not change the trading plan; instead, you are working on your personality traits to follow the plan. Strive to make minor improvements to the trading strategy weekly. The same concept applies to your day-to-day review of yourself. Work one thing at a time. Trying to solve a lot of problems at once means you are not focusing enough on each problem because your attention is spreading too widely.

They Take Action

Successful traders take action. They do not let them control their fear of their choices or interfere with their business. They use successful systems. Their methods of commercialization and metrics focus on high-probability, sound trades, managing money, keeping its strategies curve free of tying, and incorporating their program in their business plans. It is not enough to just watch videos or read. Day traders need to regularly practice what they are learning before becoming sufficiently determined to be useful in making trade decisions under ever-changing market conditions.

It is not just about putting in hours of action. Day trading is possible for years, putting in hundreds or thousands of hours and never seeing any progress because you are not focused on a particular activity.

Focus on a particular activity to practice effectively.

Here's where the intention to exchange comes in. A trading plan is a document that specifies precisely how, why, and when a trader joins and exits trades, how they control the risk, and what the size of their position will be. It also specifies which markets are to be traded and when. The practice involves implementing a plan to allow tracking of progress.

Practice day trading in a demo account, one component of the trading plan at a time, until the strategy becomes second nature. You may go through charts, for example, and pick entry points for your strategy. Do this until you see all of the entry points your strategy provides. Day trading requires fast reflexes and accurate timing. Practice so entries occur precisely when they should, depending on the technique. Then move on to putting right the stop-loss. Then practice correctly positioning the target for income. Practice having the perfect size of position on each trade and every other trading element covered by the trading plan. While it may sound a little strange, you are also learning what not to do this whole time.

Your aim is not only to take action on your strategy and take all the trades you are told to make (when circumstances are favorable, based on your trading plan), but also to practice sitting on your hands when your strategy does not ask you to take a trade. Trading is about the deals you do not carry out as much as it is about those you do. When your plan does not deliver a trade incentive, then do not do it. Most new traders lack the patience needed to wait for a legitimate trade signal, but it can be learned through practice.

Where a legitimate trade opportunity occurs, practice being cautious and pouncing. The amount of time that traders will practice will differ for every item of their trading plan. You will usually work

15 to 20 days on every item of the trading plan. Using this method, a trader should have a clear understanding of their trading plan after about six months, have their strategy practiced for days, and have a reasonable idea of how to use it under all market conditions.

They Are Disciplined

Discipline is a key trait that every trader needs. The market gives you limitless possibilities for trade. Every second of the day, you will exchange thousands of different items, but very few of those seconds provide great commercial opportunities.

If a strategy provides about four to five trades a day and stop loss and goals for each trade are automatically set. During the day, there are just about five seconds of real trading activity.

CHAPTER 9:

What Is Best to Trade?

When it comes to buying and selling stocks, it is entirely up to the investor to choose whatever he or she thinks will be a good investment. It is tough to generalize the type of stock that will suit everyone, as there is no one stock that fits all rule. However, here are the types of stocks that can be dealt with in the share market.

Company Stocks

Company stocks are those that are issued by the company to their employees and also to the public. Although top companies do not directly open up their shares for the public, employees who own the shares can sell them in the market. There are several multinational companies to choose from, including Microsoft, Coca Cola, Intel, Apple Inc., Nokia, etc. You can choose a company that you think will help you increase the value of your investment. You will have to research the companies which are doing well and which ones aren't and choose to invest in them accordingly. But don't be in too much of a hurry to find the best stocks for you. Take your time and observe the trend for a few months. Once you establish a pattern, you can start buying the stocks of that company.

Commodities

The commodities market is where several types of commodities are bought and sold. These commodities can be of the following types:

Agricultural

Agricultural commodities are food items such as vegetables, fruits, pulses, and other crops. Each commodity has a different price, and depending on which crops are doing well, you can decide to invest in them. These commodities are ideal for day trading as they generally rise in value by the end of the day. Some of the most preferred commodities include potatoes, pulses, rice, and sugar.

Metal

Metals are also a good market for investors. Metals such as copper, nickel, iron, and lead all have a good market value. It is possible for you to trade in these metals, and you will have to look for the ones that are currently doing well. You can choose to hold on to them for a specific period of time and then sell them before the deal's expiry date.

Industrial

Industrial solvents, chemicals, and other such liquid commodities are also quite popular. They are in constant demand and command high prices. You can choose the ones that you think will fetch you a good price and invest in them.

Energy

Energy resources such as crude oil, petroleum, paraffin, etc. are also traded. These are required to fuel your cars, used in cosmetics, etc. And so are in constant demand. You can choose the one that you think is in good demand and trade with them.

Livestock

Just like the other commodities, livestock is also traded on a daily basis in the stock market. These include pigs, sheep, etc. There are many factors that can affect their prices, including weather conditions, diseases, and also their market demand and supply.

These form the various types of commodities that you can choose from, and you can purchase one type or diversify by purchasing several types.

Currencies

When it comes to day trading, it is possible for the investor to trade in currencies. As an investor, you have a lot of choices and flexibility to hedge your currency exposure to risk. FX options, as currency trading in the options markets is popularly known, allow the same core hedging and trading strategies used when trading options on ETFs, stocks, and indexes. The best and most straightforward way to remember what type of "option" you need to trade on is to focus on the base currency or the first currency in every currency pair. The second currency in the pair is the quote currency or the counter-currency. "Options" prices are typically derived from the base currency and are relative to the quote currency.

A USD-based currency pair (per USD) is available for the ten FX pairs. For instance, when you expect the US dollar to strengthen against the Japanese yen, you purchase YUK calls. In the inverse situation, when you expect the yen to strengthen against the US dollar, you purchase YUK puts.

It is up to you to decide what you think is best suited to trade with, depending on the resources you have at hand. You don't need to have extensive knowledge of these products, and only a little knowledge is enough for you to know if the products are worth investing in.

Index

Index trading refers to a type of trading where you bet on the index's rise and fall. Each sector of the stock exchange will have an index, which will take into account the prices of all the stocks that are listed under that index. Then by dividing it by the number of stocks present in the market, you will get a certain number. Now all of these indexes are pooled, and a final index is prepared, which is the entire share market's collective index. Now you can "bet" on where the index will reach by the end of the day. For this, you must study the individual indexes such as the IT industry index, the consumer goods index, etc. Once you think you know where the index will be by the end of the day, you can invest in it.

ETF

An ETF is also known as Exchange Traded Funds. These ETF's are like mini mutual funds that are traded in the market. Each ETF will have a combination of different underlying securities, and these will be split into several small pieces. You can buy these in bulk, and they can be traded on a daily basis. The main idea is to buy them at a low price and then dispose of them at a higher price. You have to understand that they are slow movers, and you will have to buy them and wait for them to grow in value. These are much preferred as they will give you the advantage of a mutual fund but can be exchanged on a daily basis.

Bonds

Bonds are securities that are issued by companies and can be bought and sold to realize a profit. These bonds can come in several different forms and are explained below:

Government Bonds

Government bonds refer to those bonds that are issued by the government. As you may know, the government requires funds from time to time and will ask you to pay forward. Once you do, they will issue you a bond that is valued much lower than its actual value. After it matures, you can collect the amount you paid along with interest that they would pay you for it. If at any time you wish to sell the bond, then you can do so, and you will get paid a higher amount for it. The government might also agree to pay you a certain percentage of interest every month, and you can capitalize on this opportunity to keep your money safe and also earn a profit from it. This form of investment is extremely safe as the government will not default on paying you your due money.

Agency Bonds

Agency bonds are much like government bonds. They are run by companies that the government funds. So these can be counted as government bonds. They will pay you a great rate of interest on your investment. However, you cannot expect the same guarantee from them as you would from government bonds. You might have to invest a certain fixed sum as well. But given their success rate, they are a great option for all those looking to safeguard their money and also earn a certain rate of return on it. The same rules apply to agency bonds when you wish to liquidate them. You can sell them at a higher price or collect your sum and interest at the time of maturity.

Federal Bonds

Your local governments issue federal bonds. Just like how the central government issues bonds, your local governments will do the same. You can buy these bonds at low rates and then hold on to them. You can sell them whenever you like and earn a higher income from it. These bonds will pay you more than what your government bonds will, as your local government will not need a lot of money for a high scale project, and it will be slightly low key. This type of investment will be much better than saving in the bank, which will pay you much less interest.

Corporate Bonds

Corporate bonds refer to those that are issued by companies. As you know, multinational companies also require money for their projects. This money will raise by issuing bonds to the public. They will agree to pay you back after a while and until such time, pay you a fixed rate of interest. You can sell these bonds for a profit at any time. But you must understand that these companies will not provide you with a guarantee like your government and federal government bonds. So it will be a risk that you will be willing to take. However, if you choose a big multinational company, then you might hit the jackpot. Not only will you get paid more but also win over their loyalty. They might be willing to give you shares in their company at a discounted rate, which will be a bonus for you. You can then sell these stocks at a later date and realize a big profit from it!

Zero-Coupon Bonds

Zero-coupon bonds are extremely popular owing to their ease of trade. They are extremely liquid, and there is always a lot of demand for them. Now suppose a zero-coupon bond is worth $500. When you buy it, they will issue it at $100 and ask you to exchange it for $500 in 2 years' time. So despite it being valued at $100 now, you will get back 4 times the value after exchanging it in 2 years' time. So not only will your money be safe, but you will also be able to increase its value several fold.

CHAPTER 10:

How Much Do You Need to Day Trade?

Before you begin any business, one would want to know how much they need as capital. The same case applies to day trading. An important question that most investors would want to know is the amount of capital that is required from them. The amount of money that you need to day trade will depend on the market that you wish to invest in. Your style of trading will also have an impact on the amount of money that you need to raise.

Different markets will require varying amounts of capital. Below is an analysis of the different markets that are at your disposal and the respective capital requirements.

Capital Requirements for Stock Traders

If you are going to trade in stocks, then you need to have at least $25,000 saved up for the trading activity. You are not limited to this amount of money. If you wish to trade more than three times, you should consider having more than $30,000. When your trading account falls below $25,000, it would not be possible for you to trade. You will have to top up your account to the minimum balance required. The account balance minimum here only stipulates to traders who would wish to invest in US stocks.

You should realize that the minimum account balance required to invest in other stocks in global markets will vary. The country that you rise in might not have any minimum balance required. Regardless, it is advisable to deposit a reasonable amount that will see you earning good profits for every buying and selling activity that you engage in. Why are we saying this? There are instances where lower balances will only be eaten up by commissions and transaction costs. Therefore, you will not notice any changes in your account because of these deductions.

Lack of capital will always be a problem for most traders in the market. Insufficient capital will prevent you from taking advantage of market volatility. You might have incurred losses now, but later you could recover your money when the stocks unexpectedly rise. As such, having sufficient capital comes highly recommended.

Capital Requirements for Forex Traders

The forex market is somewhat different from the stock market. In this case, smaller amounts of capital are required. So, for a newbie like you, this should be good news. With the little capital that you have saved up, you can begin day trading in forex today. The advantage of forex is that you can exploit the leverage provided of up to 50:1. This could even go higher in certain nations. An increase in leverage implies that there is a higher risk that could be met with a remarkable reward.

Forex trading stands as an ideal choice for day trading due to its liquidity. The forex market is the largest market globally. Usually, the money in circulation on a daily basis goes up to $5 trillion. Therefore, the liquidity aspect of this market makes it quite appealing. So, how much money do you need to begin forex trading? With as little as $100, you can kick off trading. Nevertheless, a recommended figure is $500. This gives you the opportunity of buying currencies with ideal stop levels.

As you can see, this is a small amount of money which you will require to begin this activity. You cannot claim that you will make a living out of it. It is, however, important to remember that you can gradually raise capital with the daily incomes that you earn. In line with this, you should never overlook the importance of starting small simply because you are new to forex trading.

Capital Requirements for Futures

Besides investing in stocks and forex, you will also have the option of investing in futures. The good thing about futures is that you can invest in it with minimal capital requirements. There is no legal minimum balance that you should have so as to invest in futures. However, it is important for a trader to have enough capital to cover day trading margins within a particular day. A good number of brokers will require a trader to have a minimum balance of $1,000. If you are trading E-mini S&P 500 (ES) futures, brokers will demand a minimum balance of $400. This is the day trading margin that you will be limited to. Regardless of the fact that you are not limited to a specific balance, you should strive to begin with a realistic balance of at least $8,000. There are other futures that your broker will want additional margins for you to trade effectively. Hence, you ought to confirm with your trader before signing up for anything.

On a final word concerning the amount of money that you need, it is clear that different markets will require varying capital amounts. If you are running on a tight budget, trading in stocks is not advisable as it is capital intensive. On the other hand, forex gives you the flexibility of starting trading with as little as $1,000. Nonetheless, it is recommended for you to have more to warrant that you have a buffer. Futures is also a great option when working with limited funds.

It should also be made clear that it is never wise to trade with your capital at first. When working with a broker, make good use of demo accounts to trade with virtual money. Once you notice that your trading strategies suit you, you can move forward to use real money. The advantage gained here is that you can easily identify possible mistakes that you could make when using your money. As such, it saves you from risking with your hard-earned cash.

Defining Your Risk Tolerance

Aside from knowing the amount of money you will need to trade, you also should pause for a while and define your risk tolerance. What do we mean by risk tolerance? It refers to the degree of unpredictability in investment returns that a trader is willing to endure. As a trader, you ought to have an in-depth understanding of how much you can withstand the large market swings. There are times where you might panic when markets seem to be falling. In such cases, you might end up selling at the wrong time. Therefore, this is where you should be aware of your risk tolerance. How much can you stomach in day trading?

To clearly define your tolerance capacity, you should assess your past performance. Find out the worst cases where you have been comfortable incurring losses. There are several factors that could affect your risk tolerance capacity. For instance, if you have high possibilities of earning increased income in the near future, this will influence how much you can stomach. Also, if you are looking to take advantage of future securities such as a pension, then your risk tolerance rate will also be high. Generally, you will be ready to face huge risks when you are sure that you have other assets that can earn you additional income. The forms of risk tolerance are detailed as follows.

Aggressive Risk Tolerance

Traders who have profound experience in day trading would find it easy to face the risk of investing in highly volatile securities. This is influenced by the fact that they are well informed about market trends. With their expertise, they can easily predict the next trend of a particular security. Often, they can tolerate any changes in the market. On a good day, they maximize returns with the greatest risks. This is what aggressive risk tolerance is all about.

Moderate Risk Tolerance

Moderate traders will accept some risks but will shy away from securities that are too risky. In this case, they will go to markets that are less volatile. Their main aim is to minimize the possible risks that they are likely to face.

Conservative Risk Tolerance

Conservative traders are quite different from aggressive and moderate traders. Just as the name suggests, these investors will try their best to minimize risks at all costs. Traders that fall into this category are mostly retirees.

From the information provided, where do you lie? How risk-tolerant are you? You should realize that your tolerance capacity will change with time as you will learn how to cope with losses. However, it is vital that you know what works best for you right from the get-go. The significance of this is that you will prevent yourself from giving up each time you incur losses that you never expected. Knowing your risk tolerance is part of your trading foundation, which will confirm that you grow to become a successful trader.

CHAPTER 11:

Choosing What to Trade?

There are thousands of equities available for a trader to choose from, and day traders have no limit on the type of stocks they can trade; you can trade on virtually any stock of your choice. With all these available choices, it may seem like a difficult task to know the right stock to add to your watch list. This takes us to the first step in day trading, which is knowing what to trade.

Here are some tips that will help you to choose the best stocks for maximum profits:

High Volatility and Liquidity in Day Trading

Liquidity in financial markets refers to how one can quickly buy or sell an asset in the market. It can also mean the impact that trading has on the price of a security. It is easier to day trade liquid stocks than other stocks; they are also more discounted, which makes them cheaper.

Liquid stocks are bigger in volume, in the sense that one can purchase and sell larger quantities of stock without having any significant effect on the price. Because day trading strategies depend on accurate timing and speed, a lot of volume makes it easier for traders to get in and out of trades. Depth is also important, as it shows you the level of liquidity of stocks at different price levels below or above the current market offer and bid.

Also, corporations with higher market capitalizations have more liquid equities than those with lower market caps because it is easier to find sellers and buyers for stocks owned by these big corporations.

Stocks that have more volatility also follow the day trading strategies. A stock is considered volatile if the corporation that owns it experiences more adjustment in its cash flow. Uncertainty in the financial market creates a big opportunity for day trading. Online financial services like Google Finance or Yahoo Finance regularly list highly volatile and liquid stocks during the day. This information is also available on other online broker sites.

Consider Your Own Position

The stocks you decide to go for have to align with your goals and personal situation because there is no one-size-fits-all in the financial market. You have to put into consideration your capital, your risk appetite, and the type of investing you are going to take on. Let's not forget the role of research in all these. Your best bet is to read up on financials of different companies, study the market, consider the sectors that best reflect your values, personality, and personal needs, and remember to begin early. You need to be familiar with the market openings and time yourself to follow these openings. While day trading, ensure not to get emotionally attached to a particular stock. Don't forget that you are looking at patterns to know when best to exit or enter to minimize your losses and increase your profit. While you do not have to stay glued to your screen, you still need to know the earning season and what the economic calendar looks like. This will help you to pick the best stocks for day trading.

Social Media

This industry is also another attractive target for day trading as there are several online media companies like Facebook and LinkedIn that have high trading volume for their stocks.

Also, there have been several debates on the capability of these social media companies to convert their massive user bases into a sustainable income stream. Although stock prices, in theory, represent the discounted cash flow of the companies that issued them, the recent valuations also look at the earning potential of these companies. Based on this, some analysts think that this has led to higher stock valuation than is suggested by the fundamentals. Regardless, social media is still a popular stock for day trading.

Financial Services

Financial services industries also offer great stocks for day trading. For example, Bank of America is one of the most highly traded stocks per trading session. If you are looking for company stock to day trade, stocks from Bank of America should be among your top consideration, despite the increased skepticism that the banking system is facing. The trading volume for Bank of America is high, which makes it a liquid stock.

This also applies to Morgan Stanley, Citigroup, JP Morgan & Chase, and Wells Fargo. They all have uncertain industrial conditions and high trading volumes.

Going Outside Your Geographical Boundary

When trading in the financial market, you must diversify your portfolio. Look at stocks listed in other exchanges like the London Stock Exchange (LSE) or Hong Kong's Hang Seng. Extending your portfolio outside your boundary will grant you access to potentially cheaper alternatives as well as foreign stocks.

Medium to High Instability

A day trader needs to understand the price movement to be able to make money. As a day trader, you can choose to go for stocks that typically move a lot in percentage terms or dollar terms, as these two terms usually yield different results. Stocks that typically move 3% and above every day have a consistently large intraday moves to trade. This also applies to stocks that move above $1.50 each day.

Group Followers

Although some traders specialize in contrarian plays, most traders will rather go for equities that move in line with their index and sector group. What this means is that when the sector or index ticks upward, the price of individual stocks will also increase. This is crucial if the trader desires to trade the weakest or strongest stocks every day. If a trader will rather go for the same stock every day, then it is advisable to focus on that stock and worry less on whether it corresponds with any other thing.

Entry and Exit Strategies

After you must have picked the best stocks in the world, your strategies will determine if you will profit from them or not. There are several available day trading strategies, but to increase your chances of success, you need to stick to certain guidelines and look out for certain intraday trading signals.

Below, I will talk about 5 of these guidelines:

Trade Weak Stocks in a Downtrend and Strong Stocks in an Uptrend

Most traders in a bid to pick the best stocks for day trading prefer to look at EFTs or equities that have at least a moderate to high connection with the NASDAQ or S&P 500 indexes and then separate the strong stocks from the weak ones. This creates an opportunity for the day trader to make profit, as the strong stock has the potential to go 2% up when the index moves 1% up. The more a stock moves, the more opportunity for the day trader. As market futures/ indexes move higher, traders should purchase stocks that have more aggressive upward movement than the futures. With this, even if the futures pull back, it will have little or no impact/ pull back on a strong stock. These are the stocks you should trade in an uptrend as they provide more profit potential when the market goes higher.

When the futures or indexes drop, it becomes profitable to short sell those stocks that drop more than the market. The ETFs and stocks that are weaker or stronger than the market may change each day, however, certain sectors may be relatively weak or strong for weeks at a time. When looking for a stock to trade, always go for the stronger one. This same rule applies to short trades as well. As a short seller, you should isolate EFTs or stocks that are weaker so that when prices fall, you will have greater chances of having profits by being in EFTs or stocks that fall the most.

Trade Only with the Current Intraday Trend

The trading market always moves in waves, and it's your job as a trader to ride these waves. When there is an uptrend, your focus should be on taking long positions while you should focus on taking short positions whenever there is a downtrend.

We have already established that intraday trends do not go on forever, but you can carry out one or more trades before a reversal occurs. When there is a shift with the dominant trend, you should begin to trade with the new trend. It may be difficult to isolate the trend, but you can find simple and useful entry and stop-loss strategies from Trend lines.

Take Your Time. Wait for the Pullback

Trend lines provide visual guides that show where price waves will start and end. So, when choosing stocks to day trade, you can use a trend line for early entry into the next price wave. When you want to enter a long position, be patient, and wait for the price to move down towards the trend line and then move back higher before you buy. Before an upward trend line can appear, a price low before a higher price low needs to happen.

A line is drawn to connect the two points and then extends to the right. This same principle applies when short selling. Be patient for the price to move up to the downward-slope trend line, and once the stock starts to move back down, you can then make your entry.

Take Your Profits Regularly

As a day trader, you have limited time to make profits, and for this reason, you need to spend very little time in trades that are moving in the wrong direction or losing money. Let me show you two simple guidelines that you can use to take profits when trading with trends:

In a short position or downtrend, take your profits slightly below or at the former price low in the current trend.

In a long position or uptrend, take your profits at slightly above or at the former price high in the current trend.

Do Not Play When the Market Stalls

The market may not always trend. The intraday trends may reverse so often that it becomes hard to establish an overriding direction. If there are no major lows and highs, ensure the intraday movements are large enough to increase the chances of profits and reduce the risks of loss. For instance, if you are risking $0.15 per share, the EFT or stock should move enough to give you a minimum of $0.20 - $0.25 profit using the guidelines stated above. When the price is not trending (that is, moving in a range), move to a range-bound trading technique. During a range, you will no longer have an angled line but rather a horizontal line. However, the general concept still applies: purchase only when the price goes to the lower horizontal area (support) and then begins to move higher. Short sell once you notice that the price has reached the upper horizontal line (resistance) and begins to go lower again.

Your buying strategy should be to exit close to the top of the range but not exactly at the top. Your shorting strategy should be to exit in the lower part of the range but not exactly at the bottom. The chances of making gains should be more than the risk of loss. Place a stop loss just above the most current high before entry on a short signal or just below the most current low before entry on a buy signal.

Several traders find it hard to alternate between range trading and trend trading, and so they opt to do one or the other. If you choose to go for range trading, then you should avoid trading during trends but focus on trading EFTs or stocks that tend to range. On the other hand, if it is trend trading, avoid trading when the markets are ranging, and you should concentrate on trading EFTs or stocks that have the potential to trend.

CHAPTER 12:

Have the Right Mindset

Day Trading can be a bumpy road if you feel that your mental energy is no more and that you cannot focus on the markets anymore. Luckily, you can resolve this problem and start enjoying trading once again by improving your mindset. Some people opine that stock markets are generally immoral, but the fact is that stock markets are neither immoral nor moral. Stock markets lack an emotion, that's why it is up to you how you perceive the stock market to behave. If you want to enter the business of the stock market for the long term and also establish yourself as a full-time day trader, you must develop a specific mindset that aids you in observing the stock market from an unemotional point of view.

It is your mindset that will control your reactions to different transactions. It is your mindset that will help you define how you react to lost trades and big profits. Your mindset will define how you can stay calm during turbulent times and how you can avoid reacting based on emotions. A trader who is disciplined and who has a strong mindset will never let emotions meddle with his or her decisions regarding the stock market. If this sounds hard for you, don't worry because it should sound hard for every beginner. It takes a bit of effort to achieve that status. There is no way by which you can become a successful trader overnight. Trading is just like another business. As you cannot become a successful businessman overnight, you cannot become a disciplined trader overnight. You need to give yourself time to achieve the success that you are looking forward to.

Importance of a Positive Mindset

The stock market is void of emotions, but the participants of the markets are usually full of them. This is the reason reading chart patterns and trends work so well when it comes to trading. They show us some well-known patterns that humans possess. That's how as a trader you can take advantage of the market psychology. There is a notorious saying that 90% of traders lose 90% of funds in 90 days. This is wicked, to say the least, but still, this phrase is popular among traders. Before you take the leap in the stock market, you should ask yourself what are the psychological traits that 10% of the remaining traders have. What qualities they possess that make them different from the rest of the lot. If 90% fails, the money they have lost has surely gone to the 10% who succeeded. That's intriguing! Isn't it? When you lose, someone is earning your money. The people who are earning your money are humans just like you. They are a small bunch of traders who have found the secret of trading, which is nothing else but a trader's mindset. The term trading psychology refers to a specific state of mind that a trader usually has while he or she trades. If you don't have the right mindset, the odds will likely be turned against you.

Shape up Your Trader's Mindset

Day Traders can reshape their mindset by acting in a calm and relaxed manner. If you have proper knowledge of the subject and you have kept in place proper risk management guidelines, you need not be concerned about your trades at all. If a trade hits the stop-loss level, it doesn't mean that the world has ended for you. Traders lose trades all the time. It happens to even professional traders who have years of experience. Professional traders whose bread and butter rely on trading stocks have a winning rate of 50%. Even at this rate, you can bag sufficient profits on your capital if you trade with the right mindset.

You should practice the habit of not taking a losing trade to heart. There is nothing personal in a lost trade, although the temptation to make it personal runs high. The thought may start spinning in your head that you have lost something you could have easily won, or you could have easily prevented. If you think like that, the need of the hour is to train your brain into thinking that markets tend to go upside and downside almost all the time. As a day trader, you should keep faith in the market analysis that you have already done. Just stick to the plan until the end of the day. Markets are void of emotions, and if you start succumbing to your emotions, you will not be able to compete with the traders who don't let their emotions meddle in their trading transactions over the day. Try to nurture a morning routine for a more relaxed trading session. Try to wake up earlier, do some workout or a yoga session, and then sit on your desk with a heart full of faith in the homework you have done for the day.

Learn! Learn! Learn!

The education of the stock market is the key to success. It is one of the most important factors that play a key role in removing fear from your brain. This is what separates an average trader from a successful trader. Even if you have nurtured and developed the right mindset for trading, you cannot succeed until you have a solid knowledge base for the purpose. You must have a solid understanding of the reasons behind the price movements and market reactions. Similarly, I have hinted at how a market reacts to certain news and regular bonus reports. This will add more strength to your trader mindset. There are lots of concepts that are worth learning. However, you cannot learn them in a single session. You should make it a habit to internalize a concept daily so that your brain gets enough time to understand the slight nuances in the concept and to use the same during trading without having to open a book. You also can prepare and keep notes in a small diary for reference. You can form a healthy routine by consuming an hour before going to bed a good book on trading to clear out your basic concepts and bring them into practice during trading. You also can enroll in trading courses to boost your knowledge about stock markets.

The Mindset of a Successful Day Trader

Your psychology is going to be the major determining factor in bringing about the trading results that you are aiming at. Each trader keeps a unique belief system, and it is their beliefs that determine how they trade and what results they get. The traders that have a weak belief system tend to fail even if they have the most profitable and seasoned trading strategy. What is a belief system? In simple words, it is called 'The Trader's Mindset.'

When you go through psychological issues, it is in your best interest to track the issues in your brain, recognize them, and then find a cure for them. Otherwise, you cannot fix them. A psychologist recognizes the issues and then tries to cure the patient. The process of curing a problem can take longer because the patients take long to recognize the problem and accept it as the source of their downfall. As a day trader, you need to take responsibility for your problems if you want to heal yourself. Success in trading is directly proportional to a sound and operational tracking system of your brain. It also is directly linked to a successful money management strategy, sound psychology, and proper capitalization during the day. These need to be in proper sync if you want to be successful in your trading ventures. Mastering your psychology is very well an ongoing process that goes on end until you are in control of your thoughts and decisions.

Psychological Issues

The biggest psychological issue that day traders may confront is the fear of being stopped out or the fear of posting a loss and exiting a position. It is almost a nightmare for day traders, and it definitely weakens their nerves. The basic reason behind this behavior is that a trader is afraid of failure, and he feels as if he will not be able to bear the loss. His ego is well at stake. If you are getting out of a trade too early, you are losing profit if not capital. It becomes quite common for a trader to exit a position to relieve himself of anxiety and stress that an open position usually brings. The biggest fear in this sense is the fear of reversal. Traders succumb to it once it grows to an unprecedented level. They need gratification and a sense of security that their capital is safe now.

The biggest mistake that day traders make is adding on to the position they are losing. They just keep doubling down on it. This kind of act alludes to a mindset that doesn't want to accept that it has lost the game. Here again, ego won't let you close your position and save your capital. Your brain presses on winning out of the same position in which you have lost. The problem gets more intense if you have disclosed your positions to your colleagues and family members. You fear to become a laughing stock in front of everyone.

Some traders don't want to take responsibility for their trades. They cannot accept the fact that the market went in the opposite direction than they had accepted it to move. This kind of mindset fogs their brain, and they try to create a reality that is aligned with their expectations. Sometimes traders enter the gambler's mindset. They fall prey to the euphoria of a bull market and get drowned in it by slipping into gambling. The gambler's mindset always tells you to ignore the indicators of the market and compels you to indulge in compulsive trading even when the odds are against it. Trading becomes your addiction. You keep losing until your capital is wiped out. This is very dangerous, and it needs a check.

Some people start getting angry after they lose a trading position. Their brain tells them that they are victims of the trade market. There are unrealistic expectations that when the shattered result in frustration and anger among traders. This condition can strike you if you are getting too much involved in a trade. You cannot control the market and turn it in your favor just by thinking that way. You might have expected the stock to rise during the day, but markets can take an ugly turn anytime, leaving you flabbergasted. Too many expectations can lead to anger that can affect your future trading transactions. Not good for your profession. Just as excessive anger is bad for the health of your brain, excessive joy after you win a trading position is also bad. This indicates a mindset that makes you feel that you are unrealistically in control of the trade markets.

CHAPTER 13:

How to Open an Account

O nce you have your basics right and you feel primed and pumped up to invest in the stock market, you'll need your brokerage account to invest in the stock market. Without this account, you'll not be able to buy stocks or invest in other securities.

This system has got modernized, and with the coming of computers and the internet, you can make your trades in real-time through your brokerage firms. For this, you will need to open a brokerage account.

A brokerage account is an agreement between you and the brokerage firms to carry out the trades. The brokerage firm would give you software on which you'll be able to see the prices of the stock in real-time and bid on them at the price you want.

You will simply need to deposit money in your brokerage account, and through this money, you'll be able to buy the securities you want. Although the securities are purchased through the brokerage firm, you will be the sole owner of the assets, and the brokerage firm will simply charge the brokerage fee on the trades executed through it.

The process of opening a brokerage account is not very difficult, but there are several things you need to keep in mind. The cost, quality, and service are some of the things that would matter a lot for you in the end. You will also have to pay a lot of attention to the brokerage fee charged by the firm, as that can also be substantial for a small investor. You'll also need to consider the kind of securities you want to trade-in.

Choose the Kind of Brokerage Account You Really Need

As a beginner, it is not uncommon for people to get baffled by the kind of options available in front of them. The same can happen while choosing the kind of account you need.

For beginners, Robo Advisory services are the best option as they cost less, and they can help you in planning long-term based on your investment and waiting potential. The fees charged by Robo advisor services are low, and they have good algorithms to balance your funds as per your needs. Robo advisors are algorithm-based financial planning services that provide you an automated digital platform. Robo advisors would ask you detailed questions about your financial goals and also the kind of investments you can make, and based on that analysis, they will suggest the investments that can work for you. The best thing about Robo advisors is that they will do most of the work and planning for you, and hence you wouldn't need to track the market a lot. They will also carry out the rebalancing from time to time to ensure that the funds remain in good condition. They are very inexpensive, and you can open accounts with a very low balance. Popular Robo advisor accounts are Betterment, Wealth front, Personal Capital, Bloom, etc.

Alternatively, if you really want to get actively engaged in the stock market and want to invest your time in it, you can also open regular brokerage accounts where you can choose to trade in a variety of asset classes like stocks, ETFs, or Mutual funds. You can also get an option to trade regularly if you wish to. You will also have to pay attention to tax, and this brings us to the point of whether you would like to open a regular taxable account or an individual retirement account, as tax slabs vary in both. You should also consider the fact whether you want to own and operate that account solely, or you want others in your family also to have a role in it. Charles Schwab, Fidelity Investments, Merril Edge are some of the brokerage firms that provide such accounts that can be very helpful for beginners.

The Cost and Features

Brokerage firms charge fees and commissions, and there are many other costs involved that differ with every broker. The beginners should go for brokers that have low fees and more focus on educating the trader. A simple platform with better access to knowledge is always better for a beginner. Remember, you are going to invest your hard-earned money there, and you might not have much of it. This can make you feel overwhelmed when you are at the portal. At that moment, an interface that's educating and simple is always helpful. As a beginner, you should also look for brokers that have low fees.

Opening a Brokerage Account

Opening a brokerage account these days is not very difficult. Most of the things get done online, and hence there is very little paperwork involved.

However, this doesn't mean that the process of opening a brokerage account is not going to be extensive.

You'll need to fill in a lot of information for opening your account.

From your personal information like your name, address, date of birth, and social security number to a lot of other details like your IRS Tax Id, signature, annual income, net worth, and employment status will be required. You should not hesitate to share this information as it is required. You must understand that opening a brokerage account is a detailed process, as you can be having short term and long-term holdings in this account, and such information will be required. Apart from these, you may also be asked about your investment objectives, financial goals, investment frequency, and risk appetite. This is done to do your risk profiling, and this helps in the assessment of your financial goals. Based on this, you can be provided with better advisory services. You may also be required to submit an acknowledgment of owning the account and an agreement that you'll provide the information the broker-dealer needs to obtain.

You can then link your bank account with the brokerage account to transfer funds easily, and your account will be good to go.

Important Things to Consider

Commissions and Fees

There are various fees and commissions involved when you buy any stock. The cost that you bid for is not the actual cost of that stock. You will also have to pay brokerage fees, taxes, and settlement charges, and that should also be taken into consideration while calculating your actual cost.

The Brokerage Firms Will Charge You for Many Other Things Too

There are many costs involved with a brokerage account. For instance, you might get charged for inactivity fees, annual charges, fees for research and data, trading platform fees, as well as several other charges. You must have it clear in your mind the kind of charges you might have to pay at the end of the day so that there are no unpleasant surprises in the form of unexpected expenses.

Have the Frequency of Your Trades in Mind

This is also a very important thing to keep in mind. The people who wish to make trades very frequently would like to keep the commissions low. For them, even a slightly higher commission can raise the cost of the trade. Whereas, if you don't wish to trade frequently and would invest only occasionally, it might be a good idea to look at the kind of charges levied by the broker in the form of inactivity fees.

Good Support System is Helpful

As a beginner, give preference to brokerages that have a good support system as you can have frequent queries. If the brokerage firm doesn't have a good support system, you will have to rely mostly on the internet, and the advice you get there may not be very accurate or precise.

CHAPTER 14:

Tools and Platforms

For you to carry out day trading successfully, there are several tools that you need. Some of these tools are freely available, while others must be purchased. Modern trading is not like the traditional version. This means that you need to get online to access day trading opportunities. Therefore, the number one tool you need is a laptop or computer with an internet connection. The computer you use must have sufficient memory for it to process your requests fast enough. If your computer keeps crashing or stalling all the time, you will miss out on some lucrative opportunities. There are trading platforms that need a lot of memory to work, and you must always take this into consideration. Your internet connection must also be fast enough. This will ensure that your trading platform loads in real-time. Ensure that you get an internet speed that processes data instantaneously to avoid experiencing any data lag. Due to some outages that occur with most internet providers, you may also need to invest in a backup internet device such as a smartphone hotspot or modem. Other essential tools and services you need include:

Brokerage

To succeed in day trading, you need the services of a brokerage firm. The work of the firm is to conduct your trades. Some brokers are experienced in day trading than others. You must ensure that you get the right day trading broker who can help you make more profit from your transactions.

Since day trading entails several trades per day, you need a broker that offers lower commission rates. You also need one that provides the best software for your transactions. If you prefer using specific trading software for your deals, then look for a broker that allows you to use this software.

Real-Time Market Information

Market news and data are essential when it comes to day trading. They provide you with the most recent updates on current and anticipated price changes on the market. This information allows you to customize your strategies accordingly. Professional day traders always spend a lot of money seeking this kind of information on news platforms, in online forums, or through any other reliable channels. Financial data is often generated from price movements of specific stocks and commodities. Most brokers have this information. However, you will need to specify the kind of data you need for your trades. The type of data to get depends on the type of stocks you wish to trade.

Monitors

Most computers have a capability that enables them to connect to more than one monitor. Due to the nature of the day trading business, you need to track market trends, study indicators, follow financial news items, and monitor price-performance at the same time. For this to be possible, you need to have more than one processor so the above tasks can run concurrently.

Classes

Although you can engage in day trading without attending any school, you must get trained on some of the strategies you need to succeed in the business. For instance, you may decide to enroll in an online course to acquire the necessary knowledge in the business. You may have all the essential tools in your possession, but if you do not have the right experience, all your efforts may go to waste.

CHAPTER 15:

Charting

A chart is a graphical representation of the asset prices over a period. It exhibits properties like price point, price scale, and time scale. The day trader can find the price scale on the chart's right side. The scale goes from lowest to highest from top to bottom. Although it is such a simple concept, the price scale can have a complicated structure.

A linear price structure means that the space between the price points is of equal amount. If the difference between the first and second price points is 10, it will be the same for all price points. A logarithmic price structure has distances between two price points at equal percentage change. This means that if the price change is 25%, it will be the same for all the price points.

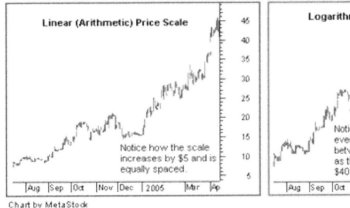

The time scale is a date or time range located at the bottom of the chart. If he opts for a shorter timeframe, the day trader can expect a more detailed chart with each data point showing the asset's closing price. Some charts can also show the open, high, low, and close prices.

An intraday chart can show price movements within a particular period in one trading session. A day trader can expect to see a time scale as short as five minutes. A daily chart can have a series of price actions with a trading session represented by one point, which can be the open, high, low, or close price.

Types of Charts

Candlestick Chart

This is a charting method that came from the Japanese. The method fills the interval between opening and closing prices to show a relationship. These candles use color-coding to show the closing points. You will come across black, red, white, blue, or green candles to represent the closing point at any time.

Open-High-Low-Close Chart (OHLC)

These are also referred to as bar charts, and they give you a connection between the maximum and minimum prices in a trading period. They usually feature a tick on the left side to show the open price and one on the right to show the closing price.

Line Chart

This is a chart that maps the closing price values using a line segment.

Point and Figure Chart

This employs numerical filters that reference times without fully using the time to construct the chart.

Overlays

These are usually used on the main price charts and come in different ways:

Resistance – refers to a price level that acts as the maximum level above the usual price

Support – the opposite of resistance, and it shows as the lowest value of the price

Trend line – this is a line that connects two troughs or peaks.

Channel – refers to two trend lines that are parallel to each other

Moving average – a kind of dynamic trend line that looks at the average price in the market

Bollinger bands – these are charts that show the rate of volatility in a market.

Pivot point – this refers to the average of the high, low, and closing price averages for a certain stock or currency.

Price-Based Indicators

These analyze the price values of the market. These include:

Advance decline line – this is an indicator of the market breadth

Average directional index – shows the strength of a trend in the market

Commodity channel index – helps you to identify cyclical trends in the market

Relative strength index – this is a chart that shows you the strength of the price

Moving average convergence (MACD) – this shows the point where two trend lines converge or diverge.

Stochastic oscillator – this shows the close position that has happened within the recent trading range

Momentum – this is a chart that tells you how fast the price changes

Free Charts

An intraday trader can use free charts that are available online and offer the trader not only with tools for technical analysis, but also with advice, demonstrations, and guidelines about chart analysis. Different free charts provide various features such as delayed futures data, real-time data, and selection of frames of time and indicator accessibility. Furthermore, these charts enable a trader to participate in various markets like the forex, futures, stock exchanges, and equity markets. Free Stock Charts and the Technician are examples of free charts that an intraday can access and utilize without spending anything.

Heiken-Ashi

Heiken-Ashi outlines use candles as the plotting medium, yet take an alternate numerical definition of cost. Rather than the standard technique of candles deciphered from essential open-high-low-close criteria, costs are smoothed to all the more likely show inclining value activity as indicated by this equation:

Open = (Open of past bar + Close of past bar)/2

Close = (Open + High + Low + Close)/4

High = Highest of High, Open, or Close

Low = Lowest of Low, Open, or Close

Regular Terms

Average genuine range – The range over a specific timeframe, generally day by day.

Breakout – When value ruptures a territory of help or obstruction regularly because of an imminent flood in purchasing or selling volume.

Cycle – Periods where value activity is required to follow a specific example.

Dead feline skip – When value decreases in a down market, there might be an uptick in cost where purchasers come in accepting the advantage is modest or selling exaggerated. Be that as it may, when vendors power the market down further, the transitory purchasing spell comes to be known as a dead feline skip.

Dow hypothesis – Average. Advocates of the hypothesis express that once one of them drifts a specific way, the other is probably going to follow. Numerous traders track the transportation area, as they can shed understanding into the strength of the economy. A high volume of product shipments and exchanges is characteristic that the economy is on sound balance.

Doji – A flame type portrayed by close to zero change between the open and close value, demonstrating hesitation in the market.

Elliott wave hypothesis – Elliott wave hypothesis recommends that markets go through repeating times of good faith and cynicism that can be anticipated and, in this way, ready for trading openings.

Fibonacci proportions – Numbers utilized as a manual to decide backing and opposition.

Sounds – Harmonic trading depends on the possibility that value designs rehash themselves, and defining moments in the market can be recognized through Fibonacci arrangements.

Fibonacci Numbers

The Fibonacci number sequence develops by starting at 1 and adding the previous number. The sum is the new number, for example: $0 + 1 = 1$, $1 + 1 = 2$, $2 + 1 = 3$, $3 + 2 = 5$, $5 + 3 = 8$, and $8 + 5 = 13$. Therefore, Fibonacci numbers are 1, 2, 3, 5, 8, 13, 21, 34, 55, 89, 144, 233, and so on.

A Fibonacci number equals 1.618 times the preceding Fibonacci number. In turn, a Fibonacci number equals 0.618 times the following Fibonacci number.

Analysts anticipate changes in trends by using four popular Fibonacci studies: arcs, fans, time zones, and the most popular, retracements. On a Fibonacci scale of 0–100%, the retracement levels within that scale are 38.5%, 50%, and 61.8%. It's amazing how many creatures in nature, human beings included, are proportioned exactly to those ratios.

Those familiar with Elliott Wave Theory know wave counts adhere to the Fibonacci numbering sequence. Many trading software platforms offer Fibonacci studies as part of their charting features. Later, I will recommend you apply the retracements to your E-mini S&P futures chart.

"How fascinating," you mutter, scratching your head. "But what's this got to do with me making big bucks in the market?"

Plenty. Especially when it comes to the numbers 2, 3, and 5. From now on, we're going to keep the numbers 2, 3, and 5 in the forefront of our minds. These numbers crop up repeatedly on charts, and we use them to help predict price movement. We'll also talk more about Fibonacci levels in later chapters.

Stocks in strong uptrends tend to move up three days, then down (pull back) for two. Or they move up for five days, then retrace for three days. In a downtrend, reverse those numbers. A probable pattern is three days down, followed by two rally days, or five days down, and three days up.

If a stock moves down for four days, you can bet it will continue into negative territory into the fifth day. (This always happens, except when it doesn't.)

CHAPTER 16:

Support and Resistance

Resistance levels are price levels at which selling pressure tends to overwhelm buying pressure during an uptrend, which can either interrupt or completely reverse an existing bullish trend. Resistance levels are usually drawn by a horizontal line that connects consecutive high prices, also called peaks or tops.

Support levels are price levels at which the opposite happens: buying pressure overwhelms selling pressure to the point that an ongoing downward trend is either disrupted or reversed. Support levels are drawn by a horizontal line beneath consecutive low prices, also called bottoms or troughs.

Significant support and resistance levels cause reversals of trends, while minor support and resistance levels only interrupt ongoing trends.

Here's how to use resistance and support levels for your day trades:

Identify your SIPs or stocks/securities in play.

Before markets open, check out the daily price charts of these SIPs and look for significant or critical resistance and support price levels for your SIPs. Always remember that support and resistance lines aren't still that obvious, and there'll be times when you may not be able to find clear lines. In such cases, don't force anything that isn't there. Just use other day trading strategies or look at your other SIPs to see if they have identifiable resistance and support lines.

When the market opens, observe your SIPs price movements using a 5-minute chart. Look for indecision or Doji candlesticks as signs for taking positions, whether long or short.

For long positions, buy at prices as close as possible to the support lines. For short positions, sell as closely as possible to

The resistance lines.

You can start closing or covering your long or short positions, respectively, when prices hit the next resistance or support levels. For optimal position management, close or cover half or a more significant portion of your open positions at the following levels. Then, close or cover the rest in the next resistance or support levels.

For long positions, set your stop-loss triggers at the support line, i.e., close your position and limit your losses when the price falls below the line. For short positions, cover your positions as soon as the price starts to go above the resistance line to minimize your trading loss.

If you're not yet very familiar with how to draw support and resistance lines, here are some tips to help you out:

You can identify support or resistance areas through the presence of indecision candles. It's because these candles indicate areas where buyers and sellers wage battles on an almost even keel.

In many cases, whole and half-dollar prices tend to act as resistance or support levels, especially for stocks priced at below $10 per share. Even if you don't see support or resistance lines on these price points, keep in mind that these numbers may serve as very subtle or even invisible support or resistance lines.

The best points for drawing these lines are the most recent.

Price points.

The more frequently support or resistance lines touch extreme price points, the more accurate or reliable those lines are. Prioritize such lines.

The only relevant resistance and support lines are those within the stock or security's current price levels. For example, it's useless to find such lines as far back when a $7.50-stock was still trading at either $13.80 or $2.45 prices. Given that you're day trading and not taking medium to long-term positions, the likelihood that the prices of your SIPs touching those levels are practically zero.

Resistance and support lines are more of estimates or areas rather than exact price points. If the support line runs through

$8.50, prices may start to bounce back within a few cents below or above this price level.

Solid resistance and support lines are those where stock or security prices have very clearly bounced back from. If you don't clearly see prices bounce back from such lines, the chances are that it's not a legit resistance or support line.

Particularly for day trading purposes, you'd be better off drawing these lines across extreme daily prices or wicks and not across places in daily charts where a significant number of price bars stopped. Why?

It's because past extreme low and high prices, i.e., tails and wicks, are influenced mostly by day traders while the price bars, i.e., the candlestick's bodies, represent daily open and closing prices that are influenced mainly by longer-term traders or investors.

CHAPTER 17:

Classic Chart Patterns

Chart patterns tell the trader that the price is expected to move in a certain path or the other after the pattern ends. There are several patterns that you need to know – reversal as well as continuation. A reversal pattern tells you that the preceding movement will turn around when the pattern completes. On the contrary, a continuation pattern shows that the preceding pattern will maintain when the pattern completes. Before you go ahead and look at specific chart patterns, you need to understand a few concepts. The major one is the trend line that is drawn to show a level of support or resistance for the commodity. A support trend line is the level at which the process has difficulty going below. A resistance trend line shows the level at which a price has a hard time going beyond. Here are the different patterns that are used by chartists:

Head and Shoulders

This pattern is a popular one and also reliable for most traders that use technical analysis. As the name implies, the pattern resembles a head that has shoulders. This is a reversal pattern that shows that the price will possibly move against a preceding trend. The pattern signals that the price will most likely fall when the pattern completes. The pattern usually forms at the peak of the upward trend.

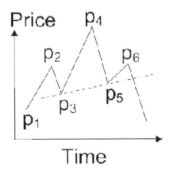

The pattern also has another form, an inverted head and shoulder facing down. It signals that the price might rise and usually forms during an upward trend.

Head and Shoulders Top

This tells the chart user that the price of a security will likely take downward trend. It usually forms at the peak of the upward trend and is a trend reversal pattern.

The pattern has 4 main stems to complete and show a reversal:

The formation for the left shoulder – comes about when the commodity hits a new peak then drops to a new low.

Creation of the head – after reaching the peak, the price retracts to the formation of the other shoulder.

Formation of the right shoulder – occurs when a peak that is lower than the peak in the head.

Neckline – the pattern finished when the price goes below the neckline.

Head and Shoulders Bottom

This is exactly the reverse of the previous pattern. This signal tells you that the scrutiny will make an upward move soon. The pattern usually comes when the downtrend ends and is considered a reversal pattern with the direction going high after pattern conclusion.

Steps include:

Configuration of left shoulder – happens when the price drops to a new minimum and then to a new high.

Head formation – when the price goes below the preceding low, then it jumps back to the previous high.

Right shoulder – this experiences a sell-off, ending at a low price but higher than the earlier one with a drop to the neckline.

Neckline – the return to the previous level forms the neckline.

This pattern is complete when the price goes above the neckline.

Cup & Handle

This looks like a cup on the chart. The pattern shows a bullish persistence pattern whereby the rising trend pauses and then traded downward, after which it continues in an upward trend upon conclusion of the pattern. It can run from numerous months up to a year, though the common form remains constant.

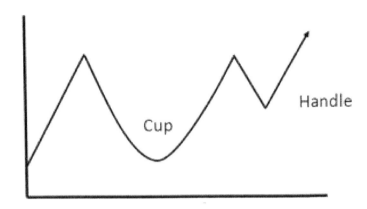

This is usually preceded by an increasing move, which then stops and sells off. This is the start of the pattern, after which the security trades flat for a long time without a definite trend. The final part of this pattern, called the handle, is a downward move that resumes the previous trend.

The Components

The cup and handle have several components that you need to know of. First, you need to know that an upward trend occurs before the trend forms. The longer the previous trend is, the lesser the possibility for a huge breakout after completion of the pattern.

The construction of the cup is vital – it ought to be nicely rounded, more of a semi-circle. The cup and handle pattern signals that weaker investors are leaving the market, and buyers are staying for the commodity. If the shape is too sharp, it shows a weakening signal.

You need to focus on the handle as well because it signals the completion of the pattern. The handle represents a descending move by the commodity after the increasing move on the right part. During the move, a downward trend line can be drawn to form a breakout. A move above the trend line shows that a prior upward trend is soon starting.

As with most of the patterns, you need to consider volume so that you confirm the pattern.

Double Top & Double Bottom

These indicate a reversal. They indicate the desire for security to continue with an existing trend. When this happens, especially with numerous attempts to run higher, the inclination reverses and begins a fresh trend all over.

Double Top

This occurs at the peak of an upward movement, and it shows that the previous trend is failing, and buyers aren't interested in the trend. Upon the conclusion of the pattern, the movement shows reversal, and the commodity is supposed to go down.

double top

The last phase of the pattern is the formation of new highs in the rising trend, after which the price starts to go towards the stage of resistance. The pattern completes when the price falls lower than the support level established in the preceding move, marking the beginning of a downward trend.

When using this pattern, it is vital that you wait until the price breaks below the key level before you place a trade. Doing this before the signal forms can lead to catastrophic results because the pattern is only setting up for a reversal. The pattern illustrates a pull between sellers and buyers. The buyers are trying so hard to shove the commodity through but are getting opposition, which prevents the rising trend from proceeding. When this continues for some time, the buyers decide to give up, and sellers take hold of the commodity, pushing it down on a new down trend.

Just like before, you need to consider volume before you make a decision as you need to look at the volume of the commodity when the price falls below a certain level.

Double Bottom

The double bottom shows a reversal to an uptrend. The pattern forms when the existing downtrend goes to a new minimum. The move finds all support, which then prevents the commodity from going lower. When the move finds the right support, the commodity will hit a new high, which in turn creates the resistance point for the commodity. The subsequent stage takes the commodity to a low. However, the commodity finds some support, and then it changes the direction. You confirm the pattern when the price goes over the resistance level it encountered before the move.

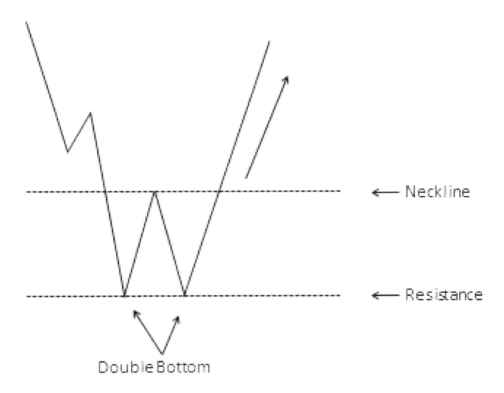

For definite reversal, the commodity needs to get the support to show a reversal in a downward trend.

Triangles

As you see from the previous chart patterns, the names leave little to the imagination. As the name goes, triangle patterns form a triangular shape.

The essential design of the pattern is when two trend lines meet with the price of the commodity moving between the two trend lines.

The triangles come in three forms – the symmetrical triangle, ascending triangle, and the descending triangle.

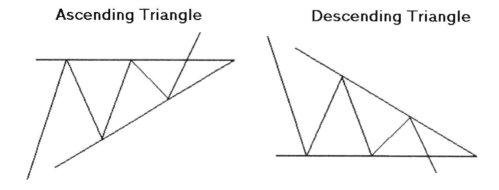

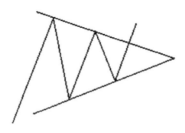

The Symmetrical Triangle

This presents a continuation pattern that signals a consolidation trend that is then followed by the continuation of a previous trend.

The triangle is formed by the junction of a downward resistance line and an equally climbing support line. These converge at the apex. The price of the commodity usually bounces between the trend lines towards the apex then breaks out towards the preceding trend.

To confirm the pattern, you need to look at various aspects depending on the direction of the pattern. If the pattern is preceded by a downtrend, focus on a break that happens under the support line.

The pattern usually completes when the stock price finally leaves the triangle, therefore look for a volume increase in the direction of the breakout.

Ascending Triangle

This bullish pattern gives a hint that the price will close higher. The pattern forms from two trend lines, one flat line that forms the point of resistance and a rising line that acts as price support.

The most significant part of the pattern is the rising support line that shows that sellers have begun leaving the security. After the sellers leave the market, buyers go ahead to push the price past the resistance level so that it resumes an upward trend.

Descending Triangle

This is a clear bullish signal. It shows that the price will move downwards when the pattern completes. The pattern comes from a flat support line that meets a resistance line that is sloping downwards. The pattern tells you that the buyers are really trying to push the price higher, but they face a lot of resistance. After many attempts, they end up fading with the sellers overpowering them, which in turn pushes the price lower.

Flags and Pennants

These are a set of continuation lines that resemble each other closely. The only difference is in the consolidation periods of the pattern. The flag resembles a rectangle while the pennant resembles a triangle.

The patterns form when a spiky price movement occurs, followed by slanting price movement. The pattern finalizes when a price breakout occurs in a similar direction to the spike.

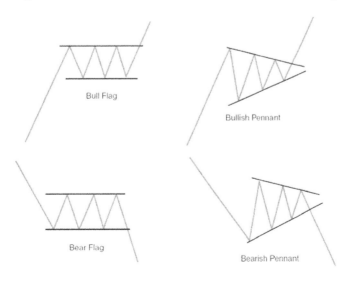

The cause of the movement is due to a huge price shift, market consolidation, or pause before the resumption of an initial trend.

The Flag

This part of the pattern forms a pattern that resembles a rectangle. This rectangle comes by due to 2 parallel trend lines that push the price until it breaks out.

The signal to buy or sell forms when the price goes through two levels, with the movement going in the previous direction. As always, consider the volume to justify the signal.

The Pennant

This is a sort of a triangle, where the lines form a convergence of sorts.

The Wedge

This chart pattern shows the reversal of the movement that forms inside the wedge. The construction is akin to a symmetrical triangle because it has two trend lines depicting resistance and support.

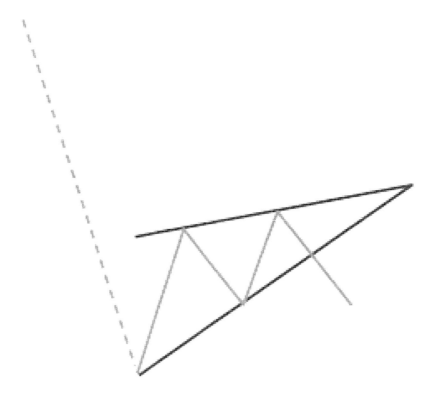

However, this pattern is different from the triangle in that it is longer, which usually lasts between 3 to 6 months. The converging trend lines incline upward or downward, different from typical triangles.

Wedges come in two types – falling and rising. The two differ due to the slant, with a falling wedge sloping downward and an easing wedge slanting upward.

Falling Wedge: this bullish pattern signals that you will probably see the price breaking through the wedge and adopt the upwards direction. You need to look at the resistance trend line, which ought to have a sharp slope than the support trend line. For this construction, the buy signal forms when the price goes through the resistance.

Rising wedge: this is the opposite of the falling wedge in that it has a bearish pattern that shows that the security might head in a downward direction. The trend lines that form this pattern usually converge, with all the trend lines slanting in an upward direction.

CHAPTER 18:

Technical Indicators

Technical indicators are tools to help traders in technical analysis of stock charts. For day trading, learning about how to use technical indicators is a very essential craft, without which you cannot become a successful day trader. This is like learning to ride a bicycle if you want to win medals in competitive cycling events. Fortunately, the technical indicators are simple and easy to learn, and anyone can find several online resources that explain what technical indicators are and how to use them.

You can also join some offline workshops or lessons to learn technical analysis. There are dozens of technical indicators used in isolation or combination by day traders. The good thing is, all technical indicators help in some way to spot the price movement and hint at the right trade entry and exit points.

Day traders select technical indicators that they like and feel comfortable working with. It is possible to become enamored with too many technical indicators and try to use many of those for chart analysis. But the best practice is to use only a few indicators and stick with those for your trade analysis.

Using too many indicators can create confusion and make your chart a jumble of crisscrossing lines. Keeping it simple is the best when it comes to using technical indicators.

Many traders depend on finding support or resistance levels for trading in stock markets. Support levels are favored for buying and resistance levels for selling. This is also known as buying low and selling high.

These levels are the most important points you will need to know on charts for the right trading. Based on market trends, different methods are used for finding these levels. Mainly, there are three types of trends in the stock market: uptrend, downtrend, and sideways trend (also called range-bound trend). In the uptrend, the price continues to climb up; in the downtrend, the price falls regularly. But, in a sideways or range-bound trend, the price moves up and down within a horizontal range. In the up and downtrend, a slanting trend line shows the trading pattern.

Trend Lines

The first tool we will talk about is the trend-line. This is the most basic analysis tool that you will ever learn about. I can guarantee that you will find this tool in just about any trading software out there. So what is it?

Based on market direction, there are two types of trend lines: an uptrend line and a downtrend line. Let us take a look at each one of them.

An Uptrend Line

As the name suggests, this is a line that is drawn on an uptrend, such as the one shown above.

In case you forgot, an uptrend is basically an upward market movement. When a market goes up creating an uptrend, it does so in a zigzag manner, creating a pattern that is composed of small troughs and hills.

The troughs are commonly referred to as support levels. Support levels are also referred to as reactions or corrections. These are points where the market retraces back a bit before advancing in its original direction. These troughs offer excellent buy opportunities.

These troughs become the touching points when you are drawing an uptrend line.

One thing to keep in mind is that the touching points must be at least three for the line to be considered a valid trend line.

A Downtrend Line

Then we have the downtrend line.

Likewise, when a market is moving downwards, it will move in a zigzag manner, such as the one shown above, creating hills and troughs. However, unlike the uptrend line, this line is drawn across the hills. These points are also called points of resistance or resistance levels. And they offer excellent selling opportunities in a falling market.

Moving Averages

The Moving Averages are slanting indicators that move with the trend line and show major support and resistance areas. These indicators consist of different periods, such as the 20 days; 50 days; 100 days; and 200 days. Day traders use moving averages to find support and resistance points while markets are trending.

On the other hand, the sideways trend is created by a horizontal movement of price. In such trends, traders require knowing horizontal support and resistance levels for buying and selling purposes. Day traders use pivot levels or Fibonacci levels in range-bound market conditions for spotting support and resistance. These are the simplest of indicators. Pivot levels are calculated by certain methods, and pivot calculators are freely available online. Fibonacci levels are drawn on technical charts from the highest and lowest price points. All trading charts provide facilities to draw Fibonacci levels.

The third most important and simplest trading indicator is the RSI (Relative Strength Index). As the name suggests, this indicator shows the strength of any trend. RSI is plotted below the main charting area and keeps rising and falling with the price moment. A rising RSI shows the strength of an uptrend, and a falling RSI shows the strength of a downtrend. It has the top and bottom areas, respectively called overbought and oversold areas. Day traders look to sell from the overbought region and buy near the oversold area.

One can combine support and resistance indicators with the RSI and plan their trading strategies for buying and selling.

Momentum Indicators

Momentum indicators show the strength of a trend and whether a reversal is likely to occur. They are very useful in finding peaks and troughs. As such, they can be useful in knowing when or where to enter or exit a trade.

Some examples of momentum indicators are the Average Directional Index (ADX), Relative Strength Index (RSI), and the Stochastic.

These indicators are leading.

Oscillators and Market cycles

These refer to indicators such as the Relative Strength Index (RSI) and the Moving Average Convergence Divergent (MACD) that reflect unclear price trends. The signals move between the upper bounds and lower ones, and the subsequent readings provide the day trader with feedback regarding the market conditions.

CHAPTER 19:

Types of trades

There are different reasons some traders love to use forex instead of the stock market. One of them is the forex leverage.

When it comes to forex trading, the entire system is totally different. Before you can trade using leverage, you need to have opened the forex trading account. That's the only requirement that is out there, nothing else. When you open a forex account, you can easily use the leverage feature.

If you are trading in the United States of America, you will be restricted to a leveraging of 50: 1 leveraging. Countries outside of the US are restricted to leverage of about 200: 1. It is better when you are outside the US than in the US. Liquidity differences

When you decide to trade stocks, you end up purchasing the companies' shares that have a cost from a few dollars down to even hundreds of dollars. Usually, the price in the market tends to share with demand and supply.

Paired Trades

When you trade with forex, you are facing another world, unseen in the stock market. Though the currency of a country tends to change, there will always be a great supply of currency that you can trade. What this means is that the main currencies in the world tend to be very liquid. When you are in forex trading, you will see that the currencies are normally quoted in pairs. They are not quoted alone. This means that you should be interested in the country's economic health that you have decided to trade in. The economic health of the country tends to affect the worth of the currency.

The basic considerations change from one forex market to the next. If you decide to purchase the Intel shares, the main aim is to see if the stock's value will improve. You aren't interested in how the prices of other stocks are.

On the other hand, if you have decided to sell or buy forex, you need to analyze the economies of those countries that are involved in the pairs.

You should find out if the country has better jobs, GDP, as well as political prospects.

To make a successful trade in the Forex market, you will be expected to analyze not only one financial entity but two.

The forex market tends to show a higher level of sensitivity in upcoming economic and political scenarios in many countries.

You should note that the U.S. stock market, unlike many other stock markets, is not so sensitive to a lot of foreign matters.

Price Sensitivity to Trade Activities

When we look at both markets, we have no choice but to notice that there is varying price sensitivity when it comes to trade activities done.

If a small company that has fewer shares has about ten thousand shares bought from it, it could go a long way to impact the price of the stock. For a big company such as Apple, such number of shares, when bought from, it won't affect the stock price. When you look at forex trades, you will realize that trades of a few hundreds of millions of dollars won't affect the major currency at all. If it affects, it would be minute.

Market Accessibility

It is easy to access the currency market, unlike its counterpart, the stock market. Though you may be able to trade stocks every second of the day, five days weekly in the twenty-first century, it is not easy.

A lot of retail investors end up trading via a United States brokerage that makes use of a single major trading period every day, which spans from 9: 30 AM to 4: 00 PM. They go ahead to have a minute trading hour past that time, and this period has price and volatility issues, which end up dissuading a lot of retail traders from making use of such time. Forex trading is different. One can carry out such trading every second of the day because there are a lot of forex exchanges in the world, and they are constantly trading in one time zone or the other.

Forex Trading Vs. Options

A trader may believe the United States Dollar will become better when compared to the Euro, and if the results pan out, the person earns.

CHAPTER 20:

Setups and Trading strategies

Anyone who wishes to make money with stock trading should have a better strategy on how to predict the trend in prices of the stock in order to maximize profits. The charts show the trends that have different patterns that a new person in the trade cannot easily interpret. The patterns in the trend have meanings that give signals to the trader on when to make a move by either buying or selling stock.

The ABCD Pattern

This is a harmonic pattern that is used to derive the other patterns of trade. This pattern is made up of three swings that are made up of the AB and CD lines, also known as the legs. The line BC is known as the correction line. The lines AB and CD are almost of the same size. The AB-CD pattern uses a downtrend that indicates that the reversal will be upward. On the other hand, the bearish pattern uses the uptrend, which means that there will be a reversal downward at some point. When using this pattern for trade, you have to know the direction of the trend and the movement of the market. There are three types of ABCD pattern: the classic ABCD pattern, the AB=CD pattern, and the ABCD extension.

When using this pattern, remember that one can only enter the trade when the price has reached point D. Therefore, it is essential to study the chart o at the lows and highs; you can use the zigzag indicator, which marks the swings on the chart. As you explore the chart, watch the price that forms AB and BC.

In a bullish trade ABCD, C should be at the lower side of A. The point A, on the other hand, should be intermediate-high after B that is at a low point. D should be a new point that is lower than B. as mentioned earlier, the entry is at point D, but when the market reaches point D, you should not be too quick to enter the trade, consider other techniques that would make sure that the reverse is up when it is a bullish trade, and down when it is a bearish trade.

Flag Momentum

In a trading market, there are times when things are good, and the traders enjoy an upward trend, which gives a chart pattern that represents a bull flag pattern. It is named as such because when you look at the chart, it forms a pattern that resembles a flag on a pole. The trend in the market is an uptrend, and therefore the pattern is referred to as a bullish flag. The bull flag pattern is characterized by the following; when the stock makes a positive move with a relatively high volume, the pole is formed, when the stock consolidates on a lighter volume at the top, the flag is formed. The stock continues to move at a relatively high volume breaking through the consolidation pattern. The bull flag momentum is a trading strategy that can be used at any given time frame. When it is used to scalp the movements of price, the bull is used only on two instances of time frame: the second and the fifth minute time frames. The trading bull flags also work well when using daily charts to trade and can also be used effectively when swing trading.

It is simple to trade, but it is challenging to look for the exact bull pattern. This problem can be solved using scanners that help to look for stocks on the upward trend and wait for them to be in a consolidation position at the top. The best and free scanners that can be used to locate bull flags are Finviz and chart mill. There are tips that can be used to indicate a bull flag. When there is an increase in stock volume that is influenced by news, and when the stock prices remain high, showing a clear pattern for a pullback. At this point, you can now check out when the prices break out above the consolidation pattern or on high volumes of stock. To make a move, place a stop order at the bottom of the consolidation. At this point, the ratio of risk to reward is 2:1, and it is the best time to target. The most substantial part of the pattern is the volume of the stock, and it is a good sign that there will be a significant move and a successful breakout. On the trend, it is also good to look at the descending trend as it gives a sign on the next breakout. This can be seen in the trend line that is found at the topmost of the flag.

When used well for trading, the bull flags are useful tools of the trade; however, things can go wrong, and therefore one must be ready with an exit strategy. There are two strategies, one is placing a stop order at a point below the consolidation area, and the second method is using a moving average that is monitored for within 20 days. Within 20 days, if the price of the stock is below the moving average, then it is time to close out the position and try out other trading routes.

Reversal Trading

Reversal trading, also known as a trend reversal pattern, is a trading strategy that indicates the end of a trend and the start of a new one. This pattern is formed when the price level of stock in the current trend has reached a maximum. This pattern provides information on the possible change of trend and possible value of price movement. A pattern that is formed in the upwards trend signals that there would be a reversal in the trend and the prices will go down soon. Conversely, a downward trend will indicate that there will be a movement of the costs, and it will be upwards. For you to recognize this pattern, you have to know where specific patterns form in the current trend. There are distribution patterns that occur at the top of the market; at this point, traders sell more than they buy. The patterns that occur at the bottom of the markets are referred to as accumulation patterns, and at this point, traders buy more than they sell.

Reversal trends are formed at all time frames, and it is because the bank traders have either place trades are taking profits off the trades. The trend can be detected when there are multiple up and down formations that are fully formed; they should be at least two upswings and two downswings indicating a bearish pattern. The swing highs of lows on the trend line depend on which reversal pattern is formed.

The highs or lows form at a similar price because the bank traders want to appear as if they are causing a reversal in the market by getting all their trades places at the same time. In the real sense, that is not the case because they appear at different points of the trend. Therefore, as a trader, you should wait for a bright and steady trend upward for you to sell in the case of a bullish trade and a steady trend downward for the case of a bearish trade for you to buy.

There are different types of reversal patterns. The double top reversal pattern is a pattern that has two tops on the chart. It looks like "M." The double top has its reverse type known as the double bottom pattern that resembles "W." The double bottom has two bottoms located either on the same support or at different supports.

Another reversal pattern is the head and shoulders; this pattern resembled two shoulders and ahead. The two shoulders are tops that are slightly below the other top that is known as the head. The head and shoulders can also be represented in a descending pattern whereby the tops become bottoms.

VWAP Trading

VWAP is the volume-weighted average price. It is a trading strategy that is simple and highly

Effective when you are trading in a short time frame. For it to work for you, you must use

Different strategies and the most common approach is the waiting for a VWAP cross above and enter long. A VWAP that is across above gives signals to the traders that buyers would be joining the market, and there would be an upward movement of price. The bearish traders might short stock giving it a VWAP cross below, thus signaling the buyers to leave the market and take profits. VWAP can also be used as a resistance or support level for determining the risk of trade; when the stock trades above the VWAP, the VWAP is used as the support level, and when the trading is below the VWAP, the VWAP is used as a resistance level. In both cases, the trader is guided by the VWAP to know when to buy and when to sell.

When doing trading transactions, trading costs are determined by comparing the price of the transaction against a reference or a benchmark, and the most common benchmark is the VWAP. The daily VWAP benchmark encourages traders to avoid the risks of trading on extreme prices of the day by spreading their trades over time. This trading strategy favors those people who use market orders to trade rather than limit orders. This is because an opportunity cost arises from delays and passive trading.

CHAPTER 21:

Step by Step to a Successful Trade

Usually, the US stocks have over 8,000 stocks on the list, but a typical day trader has access to only a fraction of them because they just fail to build a fortune due to lack of an effective trade strategy. They enter the market based on rumors and exit it empty-handed as a result. More often they play at the cost of their precious capital. Winning can be hard in the stock market if you lack discipline as a trader. You need to identify the right stocks to create a winning situation for you. Despite the presence of the learning curve, the effort to detect the right stock is worthwhile.

In this chapter, I will walk you through different steps that are involved in the completion of a successful trade.

Selecting a Broker

When it comes to selecting brokers, you have many options available. There is full service, discount, online, etc. Understanding the differences between them and selecting the ones best suited for your purposes is crucial if you wish to succeed. Another area that a lot of beginners ignore and then receive a rude lesson in is the regulations surrounding options trading.

There are not too many rules to comply with, but they do have significant consequences for your capital and risk strategies.

This chapter will fill you in on all the details.

What Broker to Use?

Generally speaking, there are two major varieties of brokers: discount and full service. A lot of full-service brokers have discount arms these days, so you will see some overlap. Full service refers to an organization where brokerage is just a part of a larger financial supermarket.

The broker might offer you other investment solutions, estate planning strategies, and so on. They will also have an in-house research wing, which will send you reports to help you trade better. In addition to this, they will also have phone support in case you have any questions or wish to place an order. Once you develop a good relationship with them, a full-service broker will become a better organization to network. Every broker loves a profitable customer since it helps with marketing. A full-service broker will have good relationships in the industry, and if you have specific needs, they can put you in touch with the right people.

The price of all this service is you paying higher commissions than average. It is up to you to see whether this is a good price for you to pay. As such, you do not need to sign up with a full-service broker to trade successfully. Order matching is done electronically, so it is not as if a person on the floor can get you a better price these days. Therefore, a full-service house is not going to give you better execution.

Discount brokers, on the other hand, are all about focus. They help you trade, and that is it. They will not provide advice, at least not intentionally from a business perspective, and phone ordering is nonexistent. That doesn't mean customer service is reduced. Far from it.

Commissions will be lower as well, far lower than what you can expect to pay for a full-service house. The downside of a discount brokerage is that you are not going to receive any special product recommendations or solutions outside of your speculative activities. A lot of people prefer to trade (using a separate account) with the broker they have their retirement accounts with, so everything is kept in-house.

So, which one should you choose? Well, if you aim to keep costs as low as possible, then select a discount broker. Only in the case where you are keen on keeping things in one place you should choose a full-service broker. These days, there's no difference between the two options otherwise.

An exception here is if you have a large amount of capital, north of half a million dollars. In such cases, a full-service broker will be cheaper because of their volume-based commission offers. You will pay the same rate or as close to what a discount broker would charge you, and you get all the additional services. Whatever additional amounts you need to invest can be handled by the firm through their wealth management line of business.

Building Up Your Watch List

There is a visible difference between a watch list and a portfolio. Before you head off to start, you should know that a portfolio is a collection of the stocks you own at a given time, while a watch list displays the securities that you own and also the ones that you have selected even if you don't have any investment in them. Watch lists give you insights into the stocks that you will eventually want to add to your personalized portfolio.

You should create watch lists based on some current factors. You also need to use your previous watch lists if there are any. They would remind you of the searches that you have done in the past and would also help you fine-tune your future searches. Go through the list more often and also plan a personal schedule of how you will be able to comb through the list and see if the stock matches your criteria. In case of negative signals, delete the stock and save your time to focus on other stocks on your watch list.

Start with the broader sets and then narrow down your stocks while you tailor them down as per your needs. If you know about your requirements, you can weed out the stocks that don't fulfill them. The key is to keep the list up to date. As the stock market reinvents itself each day each hour, you ought to reinvent your watch list in the same way.

It is the best strategy to keep an eye on the stocks that seem to be popular. Keep an eye on the upward and downward trends in the popular stocks. When you keep an eye on the rise and fall of certain stocks, you will be able to trim and tune your watch list. You will no longer be needing to enter the stocks of only the big companies. Instead, you can prepare your watch list for small companies.

While you prepare a watch list, you should keep an eye on the candlesticks, dojis, and charts. The fluctuation of prices is another element to watch for. You can build an effective watch list by collecting liquidity components in the stocks, adding scanned stock listings that meet general technical criteria. Rescanning the watch list to see which stock is ripe for investment and which should be discarded from the list after a while is also the key strategy to add to your skillset.

For example, you can say that if a stock's volume has been unattractive for the past few days, the stock should be off of your watch list. Deletion is necessary to unburden a watch list. The shorter it is, the more you will be able to keep it into consideration.

Margin

Margin refers to the number of assets you currently hold in your account. Your assets are cash and positions. As the market value of your position fluctuates, so does the amount margin you have. Margin is an important concept to grasp since it is at the core of your risk management discipline.

When you open an account with your broker, you will have a choice to make. You can open either a cash or margin account. To trade options, you have to open a margin account. Briefly, a cash account does not include leverage within it, so all you can trade are stocks. There are no account minimums for a cash account, and even if they are, they are pretty minuscule.

A margin account, on the other hand, is subject to very different rules. First, the minimum balances in a margin account are higher. Most brokers will impose a $10,000 minimum, and some will even increase this amount based on your trading style. The account minimum does not achieve anything by itself, but it acts as a commitment of sorts for the broker.

Execution

We live in an era of high-frequency trading, and the markets' smallest measurement of time has gone from seconds to microseconds. Trades are constantly pouring in, and the matching engine is always finding suitable sellers to buyers. Given the pace of the market, it is important to understand that it is humanly impossible to figure out the exact price of an instrument.

Therefore, within your risk management plan, you must make allowance for times of high volatility when the fluctuations will be bigger. For now, I want you to understand that just because the price you received was different from what was on screen does not mean the broker is incompetent.

How do you identify an incompetent broker? Customer service and the quality of the trading terminal give you access to be the best indicators. Your broker is not in the game to trade against you or fleece you. Admittedly, this is not the case with FX, but we are not discussing FX in this book. So, stop blaming your broker and look at your systems instead, assuming the broker passes basic due diligence.

When it comes to placing orders with your broker, you have many options. There are different order types you can place, and each order has a specific purpose. First off, we have the market order. This is the simplest order to understand. When you place a market order, you are telling your broker to fill your entire order at whatever price they can find on the market.

A market order usually results in faster fills, unless there is a volatility event of some sort going on. The next type of order you can place is the limit order. The limit prioritizes order price over quantity. For example, if you want to enter 100 units of an instrument at $10, your broker will buy as much as possible under or equal to $10. If they can get just 90 units under $10, then that's it.

A limit order works for a lot of traders looking to enter a position. Directional risk management depends a lot on the size of the position, so it is critical not to exceed the position limit. For such traders, this is a beneficial order. The last type of order you will encounter is the stop order. The stop prioritizes quantity over price.

Stop orders have a trigger attached to them, and once the market price hits the trigger, the entire quantity of the order is executed, irrespective of what the price is. Stop orders are very useful to get out of positions quickly. Indeed, the stop-loss order is a stop order with the 'losses in the name simply referring to the minimization of losses in case the trade goes south.

Another order you should be aware of is the Good Till Cancelled or GTC. A cousin of the GTC is the Day order. These two do not order types as much as expiry conditions for the order. A GTC is valid until the trader explicitly cancels it, while the day the order cancels itself at the end of the market session.

All in all, there are over a hundred different types of order your average broker offers you. Do not get bogged down trying to figure them all out. Institutional traders use most of them for specific strategies. To trade well, you do not need to understand a single word of what those orders are about. Stick to the ones mentioned here, and you can trade successfully.

CHAPTER 22:

Next Steps for Beginner Traders

Success in day-trading is largely based on three essential skills:

Critical Analysis - you have to assess the tension between sellers and buyers and place your money in the winning group

Financial Management - You need to practice excellent money management, or else you will lose your money in no time

Self-Discipline - You need to be highly disciplined and stick to your trading plan. You have to avoid getting overly depressed or excited in the financial markets and the temptation to make decisions based on your emotions.

Now, after reading this book, you must be in a better position to decide whether or not day-trading is really the right career for you. Remember, day-trading requires a specific mindset, discipline, and a set of skills that you need to improve in the long run.

It is interesting to take note that many successful day traders are also avid players of poker. They say that they enjoy the stimulation and speculation that comes from this game.

But you need to remember that poker is a type of gambling. Day-trading is not because it dwells on the realm of science. It requires skill, discipline, and other skills that have nothing to do with luck like gambling. Selling and buying financial instruments is a serious business. You must be able to make quick decisions, with no hesitation or emotion. Doing otherwise could lead to a substantial loss of money and also depression in some individuals who don't yet have a formidable mind.

Once you have made up your mind and you have finally decided that you like to begin day-trading, the next step is to be properly educated. You must never begin your career in day-trading using actual cash. Look for brokers that will allow you to play with simulated accounts but are using real market data.

There are some day-trading brokers who will offer access to an account that uses delayed market data. This is not the best simulator to use. You have to work with real-time data so you can make actual decisions.

The majority of simulated data software are premium tools, so you have to save money for this software. Avoid free trials since many of them are cheap platforms. Remember, if you pay peanuts, you get monkeys. Invest in your education, and education in day-trading requires an upfront cost.

For instance, let's say that you want to get your master's degree. This goal will easily cost you around $40,000 or even more. Similarly, many diploma or post-graduation programs will cost a lot more compared to the education needed for your day-trading career.

When you have a simulated account, you need to develop your own strategy. Try the day-trading strategies we have explored in this book. Ideally, you should become a master of one strategy. Reversal Strategies, Resistance or Support, and VWAP are the easiest day-trading strategies.

You only have to master a few days of trading strategies, so you become profitable in this career. Keep it simple. Once you have mastered a strong strategy, make certain that you detach your emotions when you make the trade.

Continue practicing with the level of money that you will trade in an actual account. It can be easy to purchase a position worth $50,000 in a simulated platform and watch 50% of it vanish in a matter of minutes. However, do you have the tolerance to lose this amount of money in real life?

If your answer is no, then you will probably become too emotional while you are trading and make quick decisions that will ultimately result in substantial loss. Therefore, always trade with the position and size that you will also use in an actual account. Otherwise, it makes no sense to trade in a simulator.

You can move to a real account after training with a simulator and then begin with small real cash. Limit the number of your trades if you are still learning, or you feel that you are not emotionally prepared. Continue your self-education, and be sure to reflect on your trading strategy.

Do not stop learning about day-trading and the market you want to participate in - equities, forex, ETFs, or futures. These financial markets are quite dynamic. Day-trading is quite different from what it was a decade ago, and it will be different in the next decade.

So, continue reading and discussing your performance and progress with other day traders. Learn how to think ahead and keep a progressive attitude. Read as much as you can, but still keep a level of skepticism about everything you encounter, including this book, of course.

Ask important questions, and don't accept 'expert insights' at face value. Ideally, you should join a group or community of day traders. It can be extremely difficult to trade alone.

It can also be emotionally overwhelming. It will help you a lot if you are part of a community of day traders so you can ask questions, discuss options, learn new strategies, and receive alerts and hints about the financial markets. But don't forget that you also need to contribute.

It is essential to take note, however, that if you are part of a community of day traders, you must not always follow the pack. Try to become an independent thinker.

In general, people do change once they become part of a crowd. They become more impulsive, unquestioning, and always looking for a 'guru' whose trades they can follow. They respond with the crowd rather than using their own minds.

Day-trading groups may receive some trends together but could lose if the trends reverse. Don't forget that profitable day traders know how to think on their own. Learn how to use your judgment when to pursue the trade and when to get out.

CHAPTER 23:

The Basic Tips for Beginner's Day Trading

I t's time for you to look at how the day trading process works. You could just blindly jump in, but that is a recipe for disaster. Instead, let us get you started on how to smartly engage in day trading.

The first question to ask yourself is, how big an investment are you planning on making your day trading efforts? You need to think that not only how much money you are willing to invest, but also how much time. Many investors look at day trading as an escape from their normal jobs, others see it as an answer to the uncertainties of the job market. While you may hunger to day trade full time, people do succeed as part-time day traders while working a primary job. Beginners may also want to spend some time simulating investments to get a feel for how comfortable you are with the process and how much talent you may have. Simply jumping in is not a good idea. You need to understand the investment market, learn to look for indicators that give you an idea of stock movements, and make the most of your opportunities.

Infrastructure Concerns

While it may sound mundane, spending some time on your workspace and technology can be well worth it. Day trading can be stressful, so a work area that provides quiet and privacy can be helpful. Do not underestimate the importance of a reliable internet connection and a backup method of controlling your investments in case your network goes down. These days, it is not hard to have a fast land-based internet connection while also having the ability to use your smartphone as a wireless hotspot if your main connection goes down. It only takes one network failure when you have a big investment on the line to convince you of the importance of a backup internet access plan.

Understanding the Market

It's one thing to say you want to invest in stocks. It is another thing to find out what stocks you should be investing in. Investors break down the market into different sectors, such as "retailers," "manufacturers," "utilities," "airlines," "energy," "health care," and others. Day traders can choose to target all these sectors or choose to specialize in one or more. As a beginner, focusing on one sector may be advantageous, particularly if it is one you are already familiar with.

Since as a day trader, you are interested in identifying opportunities for small changes in stocks, not long-term growth. This means you will need ample funding. U.S. based day traders need a minimum of $25,000 for their trading account, according to Securities and Exchange Commission (SEC) rules. This means you will really need at least $30,000 to have some flexibility. Keep in mind; in the U.S., you can currently leverage your trading capital by up to 400%. This means that you could control $120,000 worth of stock with your $30,000. As you learned earlier, this also means you could suffer four times the losses on your investments. Be aware that if you do not maintain your maintenance margin amount, you can receive a margin call too. In planning for your trading account, it would be better to have more funds available, since that would make more stocks available for your consideration. Remember, it is usually more cost-efficient to buy shares in multiples of 100, meaning a small investment kitty will either limit you to cheaply priced stocks or buying stocks in smaller increments than being less cost-effective too. If you can devote more funds to your trading account, you will be able to pursue more opportunities and have the wherewithal to recover from losses.

Calculating a Simple Moving Average

The moving average is a basic tool to invest or use to monitor a stock's behavior over a defined period. The investor simply adds the stock's closing price for a specific period (two weeks, a month, a quarter, etc.) And then divides that number by the number of trading days in that period. A trader will calculate a short-term moving average and a long-term moving average for a stock (actually, you will probably calculate a few more than this to get a better sense of the stock's behavior). A simple moving average can tell you whether a stock is on a rising or declining trend.

An important point for many traders is when the short-term moving average rises above or below the long-term moving average. A short-term moving average that crosses above a long-term moving average often indicates the stock is about to begin an upward trend. The opposite is also true.

One approach to using moving averages compares a specific short-term moving average (50 days) with a specific long-term moving average (200 days). If the 50-day average moves below the 200-day average, you have a bearish signal. This is known as the "Death Cross." If the 50 average moves above the 200-day average, it is a bullish signal and is known as a "Golden Cross." While it would be nice if you could rely solely on such a simple system, remember that relying only on a moving average approach is unreliable. It is better to use this information as another bit of information when making your trading plans.

Choosing a Broker

Once you have decided on your trading allocation, you need to choose a broker or brokerage. There are several online discount brokers available to the novice investor. Many will offer you their own electronic trading program. Do not be surprised to get offers for free trades and a bonus for picking their firm. Free trades and cash bonuses are nice, but make sure you choose a broker you feel comfortable with and one that checks out with your research. The biggest online brokerages include TD Ameritrade, Scott Trade, Fidelity Brokerage, Charles Schwab, Options Express, Merrill Edge, Robin Hood, Loyal3, Options House, E-Option, and others. Some like Robin Hood offers free trades, making their overhead on charging interest on margin accounts and using customer cash to earn interest. Others may offer more services or access to more investment exchanges. One thing you will not get from any of these discount brokerages, though, is personal advice. That is the purview of the traditional broker. In choosing a broker, consider the cost of trades, your comfort level with its trading program, and your ability to access the company's website. Furthermore, investigate what others are saying about the brokerage and whether it handles the investment vehicles you are interested in trading.

Buy Orders, Sell Orders, and Setting a Stop Loss Price

Not every move a trader makes must be executed immediately or at random. You can tell your brokerage you only want to buy or sell a stock when it hits a certain price. The risk, of course, is that the stock may not hit that price while you have money planned for it. You should also plan on setting a "stop-loss price," too. This is a protective move to make sure you do not get badly burned by the stock price moving in the wrong direction. Let us say you bought shares of XYZ Corporation when their price was at $4.50 a share. Based on your research, you expect an upward move by the share price and plan on selling when it reaches $4.75 a share (always have an exit price planned). Then something goes wrong. Bad news upsets the market (in general, or it affects your stock in particular), and your stock price starts dropping instead. Wisely, you left a stop-loss order with your broker, in effect instructing the broker to automatically sell your shares when their price drops to a certain point (perhaps in this example, $4.35) to limit your loss. You should know that stop-loss orders are not foolproof. Your broker still must find someone to buy the shares at that point. In times of crisis, share prices can fall so fast that they blow by the stop loss price and keep going before they finally sell, making your loss bigger than anticipated. While this is not a regular occurrence, unexpected events can cause them. The company selling the Epi-Pen recently saw its valuation drop $3 billion in a short period of time because of news about its price markup. No day trader could have anticipated this news, and even with stop-loss orders, traders who were expecting upward movement in this stock probably lost more than they expected.

Why Day Trading is the Best Way to Make More Money Investing

Day trading is one of the best methods that you can use to make money in the stock market and with other securities as well. Many people are interested in finding a way that will earn them a good profit, and none will find a better option than day trading. Not like some of the other methods that you can use out there, day trading is unique in that you can start earning profits on your very first day. While other traders may end up having to wait a few months too many years to receive a profit, a day trader is able to get into the market and earn a lot of profits in a short amount of time.

CHAPTER 24:

Day Trading Do's and Don'ts

The blind approach to day trading is bound to failure. Knowledge on day trading is not a one-day event; it's a lifetime process. Profit making on day trading is a difficult thing to do, especially for starters, because they lack discipline and consistency. Despite the difficulty involved in this venture, some practices can help raise or reduce your profit margins. It is essential for the newcomers in this industry to learn to do's and the don'ts in day trading. Even though there is no guarantee these factors will assure you success in day trading, they will help you avoid trouble to some extent. Unlike other businesses, making the right decisions in day trading has an almost immediate impact since a slight mistake here will cost you dearly. Whereas human emotion is not an essential factor in other business ventures, the success in day trading depends a lot on human emotion. To succeed here, you will be required to mold your thinking or even let go of your old practices.

Before getting into the trade market, it is essential to learn the risks involved in it. No amount of knowledge or research can make you guess the details of day trading. The best way of learning day trading tricks is by venturing into it. Whether you are in it or looking to venture into it, here are some of the Do's and the don'ts you should be aware of before taking on the trade.

Trading Do's

Have a Trading Plan

A trading plan is an important factor for both the experienced and the newcomers in the trade market. Your plan should have all the details and aspects of your trading plan. Well, without a well-constructed plan, your venture will be more of gambling than trading. To achieve this effectively, seek knowledge of how to create a good trading plan from experienced stock traders.

Be a Realist

Always be realistic about the kind of profits you expect from the trade market. Do not let greed make you lose your decent gains. Stock markets are tricky and competitive; it is, therefore, better for you to settle for small profits rather than losing out on everything. If you lose a chance, do not beat yourself up; instead, wait for the next opportunity to present itself. A slight gain or profit boosts your confidence in the stock market.

A Strict Routine Is Important

Trading is a lonely endeavor without a boss to tell you what to do or what not to do. Therefore, a strict routine will help put you overcome the challenge of self-discipline. If it is hard for you to follow a strict trading schedule, your career as an independent trader may be far from success. Therefore, self-discipline is an essential character that anyone looking to succeed in the day trade needs to have.

Never Stop Learning

Exhausting knowledge is something no human being can do or has ever done. Even though there are plenty of quick learning systems that have been put out there for new coming traders, learn the art of day trade from scratch. It will give you a better chance to succeed. It is essential that you learn the trade using your interpretation as opposed to learning it from anyone else. Even though different trading strategies that have worked for others can work for you, market conditions differ. By doing so, you will gain more confidence in your trading abilities.

Always Seek Professional Advice

It is essential to follow a given coaching program to succeed in day trading. By doing so, time for exploration will be minimized. Even though experimentation is a good practice in day trading, seek knowledge from experienced traders. Study shows that 90% of traders who lose money during their entry to the trade market do not end their careers well.

Set a Limit on Losses

Day trading is a game where profits and losses are two of the most critical factors. You cannot stay in a business where you are consistently losing your money. Therefore, it is essential for you to set your loss limit. Once you hit your limit, decide whether you want to continue trading or exit the market.

Apply Macro and Micro Idea Generation

A good marketer is quick in identifying opportunities in the market. Day trading is full of competition; therefore, it is important always to beat the biases. Know the factors to look at when identifying a good opportunity. Macro and micro factors have direct effects on the trading market. Therefore, it is essential to correlate events, drivers, and indicators affecting the day trade market.

Concentrate On Fundamental Analysis

As a stock trader, it is vital that you learn and understand your company well. Factors such as financial information concerning your company should be at your fingertips. Through that, you will ascertain the capability and the health situation of your company. An excellent investment opportunity is that which has the stock price trading below the company's intrinsic value. The fundamental reason why most traders do not rely on fundamental analysis is that most traders spend a few days in the market.

Do the Technical Analysis

This is looking at the current stock price and currency. Analyze these factors to understand the direction the stock marketing may be taking. Also, look at the historical performance and the current stock price. These tools will help you in determining the market direction.

Do Action

Once you understand the market well and you feel confident about your next move, do not hesitate to make a move. Did you know that timing can make or break your chances of making it in the stock market? Regardless of the direction of the market, it is essential for you to set your targets to take your profits as you place your limits.

Always Control Your Emotions

The pace and events of day trading can be so tiring. Its experience can be intense and often draining mentally. A beginner will find this difficult, but once you learn to control your emotions, you will be a successful trader. The two most fundamental traits that are likely to take control of you are greed and fear. If you are not keen, the two attributes will take control of you, and you are likely to fail. Do not exit too quickly when everything is going your way because of fear. However, do not also let it run too long, in case of a constant downfall, take out your profits before it all dries up.

Do Have a Limit

To maximize your profits, use the golden rule where you apply 'stop losses' and 'soft limits' policy. This means that your previous lowest point or highest point is close to stop losses. In a case where the market is moving to a position you anticipated, then it's your perfect chance to let your position move. The most important thing here is that you maximize your gains. The number of commodities and stocks should be under control. Every stock is unique in its way. Therefore, with time, you will learn the tricks, and your judgment will improve with experience.

Mistakes Are Allowed

The moment you get into the stock market, failures, and setbacks is the norm of business. A perception that only the newcomers are bound to make mistakes is wrong; even the most experienced stock traders make mistakes. A common mistake made by most day traders is the time of entry or exit in the market. Through these mistakes, you will be able to predict and execute better. As discussed above, seeking knowledge from experienced traders will help minimize your mistakes in the market. Once you get into the market, you will realize that what you experience is different from what you learned from books. The best teacher in any stock market, therefore, is an experience.

Take Note at Every Mistake As You Improve

Losing a trade is not the end of the world in the stock market. Instead, use it as a learning process. Compare what you expected in the market to what you received. Identifying the mistakes you committed and the underlying factors that might have contributed to your failure.

Don'ts in Day Trading

Do Not Take Huge Risks

Avoid greed at all costs when it comes to day trading. Before taking any risk, look at the possibility of losing the money. If you cannot cope with the possibility of losing, then it is not worth investing your money. Always keep in mind that even with the best strategies, the chances of winning investment in a stock market is 50/50. Also, take time to learn the exact ratios that apply in the stock market since they fluctuate from time to time.

Don't Invest With The Intention Of Revenge

As a human being, you are likely to respond to an inevitable failure with a vengeance. Never approach day trade with such a plan since you are likely to fail terribly. In case of a failure, sit back and study to know the cause of your failures. Take time to strategize your next move. I can assure you that getting into the market with an intention of revenge will cause you more harm than good.

Do Not Trade Too Many Times

It is advisable for you to trade once in a while. Only put on an investment when an excellent opportunity presents itself. Proper analysis is important before putting your money on any stock market. However, you can spend as much time as you can analyze the market situation instead of doing the actual trading. Quit spending too much time trading since it is a recipe for disaster.

Do Not Scalp If You Are New In the Market

Scalping is merely taking a short cut by taking on trades that last only for a few seconds. Even though scalping is a good way of making good money, it is precarious. You need a certain level of skill and experience to understand and predict a sudden shift in market movements. In every trade you take, you are required to pay a spread fee notwithstanding the direction taken by any trade. Therefore, experience and knowledge are essential since you have got to achieve pips above the spread cost.

It is important to take notes as you try different strategies. Stock marketplace, experience, and knowledge are the two most important factors.

Do Not Trust Unreliable Sources of Information

Often you receive emails, text messages, or advertisements claiming a good profit on any stocks. Not that you shut down such sources, ensure the information they give is authentic and reliable. As a good trader, be careful not to fall into the hands of brokers who are hungry for commotions. These people can easily land you into bad trade hence losses.

Keep Away From Penny Stocks

As a starter in day trading, penny stocks should be the last thing you should do. Experienced traders will tell you that you should not engage in a trade that is difficult to exit. Also, penny stocks are highly illiquid; hence your chances of hitting huge profits are low.

Do Not Refuse To Take Out Your Profits

It natural for any human being to want more or never get satisfied with whatever they have since everyone is in business to make an extra coin. Moreover, a mistake comes in when you want to make quick money.

As a result, every trader wants to make unimaginable profits with their first trade. However, in the stock market what looks like a huge gain could end up being a huge loss. Well, expecting a huge gain from your trade is not bad. However, it is essential to be realistic about the kind of profits you expect from your investment.

CHAPTER 25:

Common Day Trading Myths You Should Be Aware Of

In the digital world we live in, it is never wise to listen to everything that you hear. Some information delivered over the internet is simply meant to blind you from reality. Other facts are there to mislead you. With regards to day trading, there are certain myths that have been there for years now. Some of these myths are just stories meant to deter people from earning profits through this lucrative trading activity. If you are new to trading, it is essential for you to know some of these myths and ways in which you could distinguish them from the truth. This section unveils common myths that you might have heard about day trading.

Day Trading is Similar to Gambling

A huge misconception that most people have in mind about day trading is thinking that this activity is similar to gambling. If you mention this to an experienced investor, the chances are that they might punch you in the face. This is because this myth is far from the truth. Day trading is not gambling. Gambling is purely based on luck. On the other hand, trading will depend on your rationality and reason. You have to set your emotions aside to ensure that you successfully trade. Also, you should realize that with day trading, there are no fast profits to expect. Contrarily, this is what most gamblers expect from their gambling activity. You need to get it clear that trading is not similar to gambling. Don't be swayed to believing that this is true.

It Is a Man's Game

You shouldn't be surprised if you come across such a myth. Trading is not something that only men can engage in. Many traders out there are women. Just because you think that there is a huge risk tied to day trading doesn't mean that it's a man's game. No! In fact, there are traders who often argue that the best investors in day trading are women. So don't make assumptions based on hearsay.

You Will Lose Everything

Honestly, how can you lose everything when you are using the risk management tips which have been discussed in this manual? Most people who fail in day trading enter the market without any plan. Also, a good number of them allow their emotions to get the most out of them. As a result, they end up making decisions that affect their finances terribly. It could also be that they lack disciple to stick to their strategies. Having a strategy is not just enough to guarantee that you limit your losses and grow your profits. You need to walk the talk by implementing the plan.

Stops Are Not Necessary

Some might lead you into believing that the idea of using stops only shows that you are too afraid to take risks. Well, this is also far from the truth. The truth of the matter is that stops are tools that help to save you from losing all your capital in a single mistake that you make. Sometimes it is better to live to fight tomorrow. Hence, you need always to embrace the idea of using stops at all times.

Trading All Day Makes Your Earn More Money

From the different strategies which you will be implementing, you will realize that there are good and bad times to trade. Hence, it is basically unreasonable to think that one could make more money trading all day. Most traders prefer to trade in the morning since they could take advantage of high market volatility during these periods.

Others prefer to trade at different times. So, trading all day does not guarantee you make more money. As a matter of fact, you could feasibly take on more losses since there is no guarantee in day trading.

Allowing Your Wins to Run

Day trading newbies will believe that the best way of making a fortune from their good trades is by allowing them to continue running. One thing that should be made clear is that you can only make money once you sell the securities you are trading.

Therefore, allowing your wins to run is not safe. Anything can happen when market prices fall drastically. It could be worse when you had stepped outside for a break waiting to make a fortune from your investments. For that reason, you should always acknowledge the importance of taking profits where necessary. Don't be greedy.

Leverage is bad

Some traders who have failed in the industry would argue that leverage is bad. Certainly, if you use leverage for all the wrong reasons, it will have a detrimental effect on your trading business. Essentially, leverage is a tool that helps you purchase more securities without funds. Therefore, if you employ a good strategy to trade, you could end up making a lot, thanks to leverage from your trader.

One Must Have a Huge Bankroll

Clearly, from what has been discussed, there are varying amounts of capital that you will require depending on the market you choose to trade. This means that the myth of having a huge bankroll for you to trade doesn't apply. With as little as $1,000, you can begin online trading. You should, however, be careful when limiting yourself to a certain amount. If you want to earn good returns, you have to be willing to risk.

You Don't Need Any Rules

Another misconception which you will come across is that you don't need to stick to any day trading rules. Picture a scenario where a soccer game is played without any rules. Undeniably, this would be utterly confusing. Day trading is just the same. Without rules, you will only incur losses. Ultimately, you will give up the perception that day trading doesn't work. Therefore, it is vital for you to have rules which help you to maintain your discipline.

Knowing that there are several myths that could deter you from knowing the truth about day trading is significant. With some in-depth research into this topic, you will garner a deeper understanding of the possible benefits which could accrue as you trade. Don't believe anything that you hear. Always make sure you do your homework before entering any trading market.

CHAPTER 26:

Common Mistakes to Avoid

Focusing on the Fundamentals

When you are first learning the basics of day trading, it is likely that you focused heavily on the fundamentals when it came time to learn which propositions were worthwhile and which were as likely to result in a loss as a gain. As you look to continue honing your skills, however, it is important to understand that the fundamentals don't matter nearly as much as the current trends the market is following.

Regardless of the individual facts, if the market is trending downward, then this affects the good picks as well as the bad. The sooner you start seeing the forest for the trees, the sooner you will start making significantly fewer losing trades. Focus exclusively on the signs you see, not on whether or not they line up with what you expect to happen. Remember, trade mechanically whenever possible.

Walking Away from an Open Position

When you were only trading haphazardly, you might have been able to get away with walking away from the action in the midst of an open trade. If you ever hope to get past average, you need to train yourself to stop that habit now. Massive swings in price can happen in an instant once the major players decide to make a move. As such, if you choose to go and make a sandwich at the wrong moment, you could come back to find that those hunger pains just cost you dearly. Day trading is an extremely risky proposition, and you must learn to treat it as such if you ever hope to see any true success in the field.

Following Instead of Learning

When you first start trading regularly, you will most likely want to look for a mentor to show you the ropes when it comes to day trading with a purpose. This is a great idea and one that is highly recommended as long as you use the resources your mentor provides appropriately. This means that while you want to follow what your mentor tells you, you will want to take the time to learn the reasons why certain moves are a good idea, instead of blindly following in your mentor's footsteps.

While both can often result in the same amount of financial gain, taking the time to understand the theory, as well as the practice, can ultimately lead you to a more prodigious output in the long run. You should set a limit on the amount of time you plan to spend with the potential mentor and strive your hardest to become self-sufficient by that time, any longer, and you may find the experience limiting instead of helpful.

Limiting Your Options

While focusing primarily on the short-term markets will likely result in the most consistent returns, thinking of yourself exclusively as a day trader is a good way to limit your overall investment potential. While it is perfectly fine to focus on day trading a majority of the time, having an unwillingness to go outside that time frame is only going to prevent you from turning a good trade into a great one.

In addition, if you are currently working with the 5-minute charts, you should consider trying the 30-minute charts instead. This does not increase your risk dramatically when compared to the 1 or 5 minute charts and actually decrease your risk as you are able to more clearly see where trends are actually developing instead of simply reacting to noise. If you feel that you have a real edge while trading in the 1-minute arena, do yourself a favor and try a weightier chart for a few days, you will be surprised at how much of a positive difference it can really make.

As you improve your skills, you should be more and more interested in what the overall market trend is and less and less on individual scalping trades. While there is certainly money to be made in these scenarios, the odds are roughly the same as winning the lottery, not nearly what you can hope to see when you simply use a reliable system and choose the right times to use it. The higher probability is the right choice 100 percent of the time.

As you should not limit yourself to a specific time table, limiting yourself to a single market a recipe for lost profits. While it might initially make sense to stick to a single market as it is the one you know the best, if you ever hope to be more than a casual trainer, then you have to eventually step outside your comfort zone and start trading based on available opportunity, regardless of the market in question.

Remember, whatever program you are using is likely connected to all the markets at once, giving you an advantage that many more entrenched traders don't have. This goes along with learning to see the wide trends around the world, regardless of the market they occur in, if you follow a positive trend across multiple markets, there's no reason it can't continue to be profitable. Get the most from your research, follow your opportunities wherever they may happen to present themselves.

Using a Gimmick

Despite the perfunctory cautionary warnings related to the inherent volatile nature of the market, many people still think that they have the magic bullet that will separate them from the pack. Unfortunately, there are no guaranteed systems or gimmicks when it comes to day trading successfully. Don't waste your time looking for one and instead invest that time in finding the most reliable system you can track down. This still won't result in a guaranteed success rate, after all nothing is perfect, but it is guaranteed to be significantly more worthwhile than chasing a day trader fairy tale.

CHAPTER 27:

The Rules of Day Trading

Let us turn our focus to some of the rules of day trading that every investor should follow. These rules are not necessarily set in stone. You can decide to take these rules with you on your investing journey or ignore them. However, they should be followed in order to give you the best day trading experience from the very first day of your investing career.

Day Trading is a Serious Business

When some people start day trading, they think that it is meant to be fun and games and do not take the profession seriously. This can be a grave mistake. While you want to enjoy what you are doing, you always want to remember that it is a serious business.

There are some types of investing that are easier to handle as a side career or on the weekends. If this is the type of investing you are looking for, you will not want to look at day trading. This type of investing is meant to be a daily business, and many people look at it as their day job. This means that once you decide to become a day trader officially, you need to treat it as you would any other career. You must get up in the morning, get ready for your day, and make sure you are ready to work by your set time, which could be as early as 7 in the morning.

While you will have some flexibility in your schedule from a regular job, meaning you could set a bit of a later start time in the morning, you will want to make sure to set a schedule you will follow at least Monday through Friday. Even working from home, you will want to make sure to limit distractions. For example, you will not want to focus on day trading and watching television at the same time. Set up an office for yourself and pay attention to your work. Get ready for your job as a day trader like you would for your job at any other office. Do not head into your office in your pajamas. You are more likely to feel like you want to put in 100% effort and succeed if you treat this as a career.

Day Trading Will Not Help You Get Rich Quickly

You should not look at day trading as a get rich quick arrangement. This is a common misconception and one reason people often turn to day trading. If you truly want to become a successful day trader, you will need to make sure you not only have the patience to build your investments, but also realize it takes time.

Day Trader is Harder Than It Looks

Day trading is not as easy as it looks, but this does not mean that you should set this book down and decide not to become a day trader. It just means that you will probably need to spend more time learning about day trading than you initially thought. You want to make sure you are well-versed in the field before you make your first investment. Luckily for you, this is one of the reasons I decided to write this book. I want to give you a comprehensive beginner's guide so you can learn as much as you can about day trading to start your journey in one location. In other words, I have done most of the research for you.

Trading is Different from Investing

One of the biggest rules that you should understand before becoming a day trader is this is different from investing. In order to help you understand the difference, here are a few basic differences between trading and investing:

As an investor, you need to have an idea where the stocks are heading in the future. However, as a day trader, you only need to concern yourself with which stocks will give you the best financial gain on that day. You look more closely at the minutes. In fact, you will not even pay much attention to the hours and will not worry about the next day, week, month, or year.

You Will Not Win Every Trade

It does not matter how experienced you become as a day trader, there will still be days that you lose on a trade. Many people create an image in their mind where they will become so experienced at trading that they will never make a mistake, and they will only gain capital.

Every game has its rules and regulations, and day trading is not any different. In case you are new to the game, you must bear in mind the entire standard rules that have been put in place to control the game. That being said, it is important to note that these rules not unbreakable, but they can be instrumental in making decisions in regard to day trading.

There are numerous rules of day trading that you have to familiarize yourself with irrespective of whether you specialize in forex, stocks, options, cryptocurrency, or futures. If you fail to abide by some of the rules, it can result in significant losses.

In as much as some rules differ depending on where you are located as well as the size of your trade, this will focus on the most important rules. In addition, it will equally discuss the rules that novices can put into practice as they venture into the complicated field of day trading. These rules will also aid the experienced traders to improve their performance in trade, for instance, in the area of risk management.

Rules for Beginners

If you are new in this field, the rules of day trading that have been tackled below can help you harvest commendable profits and avoid incurring significant losses.

Get In, Exit and Escape

One major mistake that beginners make is jumping into the arena without a well thought out game plan. Do not dare to press the "enter" button if you do not have a plan of how to get in and exit. It is understandable that some elements of excitement can set in when you are new in the field. However, it is important to note that if you do not have a formidable plan, you will be thrown out of the game completely. Make use of the rules of risk management as well as stop-losses cut down losses.

Timing

I bet you usually wake up early and bright, ready to face the day ahead in the day trading arena. However, avoiding the first quarter-hour when the market is opened is arguably one of the most crucial trading rules to abide by. Most of the activity that takes place at this time involves market orders or panic trades from the previous night. You should instead use this period to follow up on reversals. The most experienced day traders also avoid the first quarter-hour.

Be Conscious of Margin

Do you remember the days when you started off, and you were looking for capital? It was very easy to fall for a margin. However, you should keep in mind that it is a loan. A loan that needs to be repaid. In as much as it can greatly revamp your profits, it also has the ability to leave you nursing significant losses. Therefore, it is advisable to learn how to trade accordingly before resorting to the margin.

Demo Accounts

You have a lot to learn and absolutely nothing to lose by taking the initiative to first practice using a demo account. You can nurture your craft with a lot of time and space for trial and error because you are being funded by money that has been simulated. Very many brokers will give you free accounts so that you can practice because they are the best place to learn about strategies, patterns, and charts, as well as the quarter-hour day trading practice.

Learn to Accept the Loss

Virtually all the veteran traders have all achieved what they have achieved because they were willing to lose and learn from it. Losing is just the pathway to get more experience, embrace it.

That being said, it is also important to say that cutting down your losses is very important.

Take in Everything

One veteran once said that a great trader is similar to an athlete, he might possess, but he has to train himself on how to use them. Complacency should not be something that great traders relate to because they should always be; I am searching for that edge. This means that they resort to a wide range of resources to boost their knowledge. They can use anything, ranging from videos, books, blogs, and forums.

Do an Evaluation of Tips

It is normal to get excited when you are given a tip that is thought-provoking. Nonetheless, unconfirmed tips from relatively undependable sources can result in significant losses. Jesse Livermore, a trader, said that experience had taught him a tip or a number of tips that will make him more money than what his judgment can. Therefore, ensure that you double-check any information that may affect your decisions as a trader.

Rules of Risk Management

The rules of money management and the risks of day trading are key determinants of how prosperous a trader will be. In as much as you do not have to follow these rules to the letter, they have proven to be indispensable to many.

1% Risk Rule

Here, the idea is to bar you from trading beyond your ability. When you put this technique into use, irrespective of whether a trade subsidy or not, you will always have some reserve I am stacked in the bank to help you correct your balance later on.

The idea is that you should never engage in trade with more than 1% of your total account on one trade. For example, if your account has $50,000, you will only use up to $500 on your trade.

CHAPTER 28:

Power Principles to Ensure a Strong Entry into Day Trading Options

I cannot stress this enough - you need to have a plan if you want to be successful at day trading options. You are putting your money on the line every day. I am sure squandering those hard-earned funds is not the plan, but that is exactly what will happen without a proper plan in place.

Power Principle #1 – Ensure Good Money Management

Money is the tool that keeps the engine of the financial industry performing in good working order. It is essential that you learn to manage your money in a way that works for you instead of against you as an options day trader. It is an intricate part of managing your risk and increasing your profit.

Money management is the process whereby monies are allocated for spending, budgeting, saving, investing, and other processes. Money management is a term that any person with a career in the financial industry, and particularly in the options trading industry, is intimately familiar with because this allocation of funds is the difference between a winning options trader and a struggling options trader.

Below you will find tips for managing your money so that you have maximum control of your options day trading career.

Money Management Tips for Options Traders

Define money goals for the short term and the long term so that you can envision what you would like to save, invest, etc. Ensure that these are recorded and easily accessed. Your trading plan will help you define your money goals.

Develop an accounting system. There are a wide range of software that can help with this, but it does not matter which one you use as long as you are able to establish records and easily track the flow of your money.

Use the position sizing to manage your money. Position sizing is the process of determining how much money will be allocated to entering an options position. To do this effectively, allocated a smart percentage of your investment fund toward individual options. For example, it would be unwise to use 50% of your investment fund on one option. That is 50% of your capital that can potentially go down the drain if you make a loss in that position. A good percentage is using no more than 10% of your investment fund toward individual option positions. This percentage allocation will help you get through tough periods, which eventually happen without having all your funds being lost. Never, ever invest money that you cannot afford to lose. Do not let emotion override this principle and cloud your judgment. Spread your risks by diversifying your portfolio. You diversify your portfolio by spreading your wealth by investing in different areas, add to your investments regularly, being aware of commissions at all times, and knowing when to close a position.

Power Principle #2 – Ensure that Risks and Rewards Are Balanced

To ensure that losses are kept to a minimum and that returns are as great as they can be, options day traders should use the risk/reward ratio to determine each and to make adjustments as necessary. The risk/reward ratio is an assessment used to show profit potential in relation to potential losses. This requires knowing the potential risks and profits associated with an options trade. Potential risks are managed by using a stop-loss order. A stop-loss order is a command that allows you to exit a position in an options trade once a certain price threshold has been reached. Profit is targeted using an established plan. Potential profit is calculated by finding the difference between the entry price and the target profit. This is calculated by dividing the expected return on the options investment by the standard deviation. Another way to manage risks and rewards is by diversifying your portfolio. Always spread your money across different assets, financial sectors, and geographies.

Power Principle #3 – Develop a Consistent Monthly Options Trading System

The aim of doing options trading daily is to have an overall winning options trading month. That will not happen if you trade options here and there. You cannot expect to see a huge profit at the end of the month if you only performed 2 or 3 transactions. You need to have a high options trading frequency to up the chances of coming out winning every month. The only way to do that is to develop a system where you perform options trades at least 5 days a week.

To have consistently good months, you need to develop strong daily systems that keep your overall monthly average high. Therefore, creating a daily options trading schedule is key. Here is an example of an efficient options day trading schedule:

Perform market analysis. This needs to be done before the markets open in the morning. That means that the options day trader needs to get an early start on the day. This entails checking the news to scan for any major events that might affect the markets that day, checking the economic calendar, and assessing the actions of other day traders to assess volume and competition. Manage your portfolio. The way that an options day trader does this is dependent on the strategies that he or she implements, but overall, it is about assessing positions that you already have or are contemplating for efficient management of entry and exits that day. It also allows for good money management. Enter new positions. After assessing the market and fine tuning your portfolio, the next step is to enter new trades that day. Research and efficient decision-making go into this step. The options trader who has already determined how the market was doing and forecasted for performance that day would have noticed relevant patterns. The key here is to enter trades frequently via a sound strategy. To narrow done which positions you would like to pursue, keep an eye on the bullish, bearish, neutral, and volatile watch lists, and run technical scans. Incorporate learning during the day. Continual learning is something that an options trader needs to pursue, but this does not always have to be in the way of formal classes or courses. You can up your knowledge of options and day trading by following mentors, reading books, listening to podcasts, reading blogs, and watching videos online. Such activities are easy to incorporate into your daily routine. Even just a few minutes of study a day can considerably up your options day trading game in addition to stimulating your mind. Being in regular contact with other options day traders is also a great way of increasing your information well.

Power Principle #4 – Consider a Brokerage Firm That is Right for Your Level of Options Expertise

There are four important factors that you need to consider when choosing a broker, and they are:

- The requirements for opening a cash and margin account.

- The unique services and features that the broker offers.

- The commission fees and other fees charged by the broker.

- The reputation and level of options expertise of the broker.

Let's take a look at these individual components to see how you can use them to power up your options day trading experience.

Broker Cash and Margin Accounts

Every options trader needs to open a cash account and margin account to be able to perform transactions. They are simply tools of the trade. A cash account is one that allows an options day trader to perform transactions via being loaded with cash. Margin account facilitates transactions by allowing that to borrow money against the value of security in his or her account. Both of these types of accounts require that a minimum amount be deposited. This can be as few as a few thousand dollars to tens of thousands of dollars, depending on the broker of choice. You need to be aware of the requirements when deliberating, which brokerage firm is right for you.

Broker Services and Features

There are different types of services and features available from different brokerage firms. For example, if an options trader would like to have an individual broker assigned to him or her to handle his or her own account personally, then he or she will have to look for a full-service broker. In this instance, there minimum account requirements that need to be met. Also, commission fees and other fees are generally higher with these types of brokerage firms. While the fees are higher, this might be better for a beginner trader to have that full service dedicated to their needs and the learning curve.

On the other hand, if an options trader does not have the capital needed to meet the minimum requirements of a full-service broker or would prefer to be more in charge of his or her own option trades, then there is the choice of going with a discount brokerage firm. The advantage to discount brokerage firms is that they tend to have lower commissions and fees. Most internet brokerage firms are discount brokers.

Other features that you need to consider when choosing a brokerage firm include:

- Whether or not the broker streams real-time quotes.

- The speed of execution for claims.

- The availability of bank wire services.

- The availability of monthly statements.

- How confirmations are done, whether written or electronic.

Commissions and Other Fees

Commission fees are paid when an options trader enters and exits positions. Every brokerage firm has its own commission fees set up. These are typically developed around the level of account activity and account size of the options trader.

Broker Reputation and Options Expertise

You do not want to be scammed out of your money because you chose the wrong brokerage firm. Therefore, it is important that you choose a broker that has an established and long-standing reputation for trading options. You also want to deal with a brokerage firm that has great customer service, that can aid in laying the groundwork for negotiating reduced commissions and allows for flexibility. Options trading is a complex service, and your brokerage firm needs to be able to provide support when you are handling difficult transactions.

A list of reputable online brokerage firms includes:

- E*TRADE

- Options press

- Scottrade

- Ameritrade

- Train Station

Power Principle #5 – Ensure That Exits Are Automated

Even though I have stated that emotions should be set aside when trading options, we are all human, and emotions are bound to come into the equation at some point. Knowing this, it is imperative that systems be developed to minimize the impact of emotions. Having your exits automated is one such step that you can take to ensure that emotions are left out when dealing with options day trading. Using bracket orders facilitates this.

A bracket order is an instruction given when an options trader enters a new position that specifies a target or exit and stop-loss order that aligns with that. This order ensures that a system is set up to record two points – the target for profit and the maximum loss point that will be tolerated before the stop-loss comes into effect. The execution of either order cancels the other.

Glossary

Some common trading terms you will come across while day trading.

A

Ask

Ask price is what a seller offers to a buyer for selling any financial asset.

B

Broker

A broker can be an individual or a firm that acts as an intermediary between traders and exchanges and receives a commission whenever a trade is executed between these two parties.

Bid

In day trading, bid price is what a buyer offers to a seller for purchasing any financial asset.

Bear

Traders who have a negative outlook on markets, and expect the price to fall, are called bears.

Bear Market

In a bear or a bearish market, the price trend continuously declines.

Bull

Traders who have a positive outlook on the market, and expect the price to rise, are nicknamed bulls.

Bull Market

Markets with the rising price pattern are called a Bull market.

C

Cash Market

A market where actual stocks and commodities are traded.

Call Option

Options contracts that are bullish on markets. Popular among day traders.

D

Daily Trading Limit

Exchanges set the maximum price range each day for any contract. The daily trading limit does not mean that it will halt the trading, but only places a limit on the movement of price.

Day Order

An order placed during an intraday session, valid only for that session. It automatically gets canceled when the session closes.

Day Trade

Buying and selling of financial assets on the same day. These assets can be stocks, commodities, forex, or options.

Day Traders

Traders who buy or sell financial assets through a single session and close all their positions before the end of the day. They do not carry forward their positions for the next session.

E

Exchange

A regulated central marketplace where buyers and sellers trade financial assets.

F

Futures

Derivative contracts that cover the buying and selling of financial assets for future delivery. These trades take place on a future exchange.

Futures Contract

These are derivative agreements conducted through a futures exchange. These are legally binding on traders who buy or sell financial instruments for future delivery. Futures contracts have standard regulations based on quantity and delivery time.

G

Good till Canceled (GTC)

Open orders with buying or selling instructions at a specific future price and can remain open till the order is executed.

H

Hedge

The simultaneous buying and selling of a derivative contract of a later date. This is done to balance a loss and profit of open positions in derivatives and cash markets.

Hedger

When companies or individuals, who are holding positions in cash markets, make an opposite trade in the derivatives markets to balance any potential loss, they are called hedgers.

Hedging

The act of balancing any potential risk of loss in cash markets by taking an equal but opposite position in the derivative markets.

I

Initial Margin

To open a new position in derivative markets, such as in futures and options, traders are required to deposit a minimum amount of money in their trading accounts, called initial margin. This is to mitigate any risk of loss because of market volatility. The level of initial margin can increase or decrease according to the market volatility.

L

Last Trading Day

The last trading day is not the last day of the month, but the last trading day of derivative contracts (futures & options). On this trading day, the monthly derivative contracts are settled among traders.

Limit Order

An order, given to buy or sell a financial instrument at a specific price, beyond which the order is not filled. This shows that the buyer or seller will trade only at a specific price.

Liquidity

A characteristic of tradable financial instruments, which shows the ease of trading those. Traders and investors prefer to buy or sell highly liquid assets because these can be easily bought or sold.

Long

A trader is supposed to be 'long' if he has a bullish outlook for the market. A long position is taken when buyers expect the price to rise.

M

Maintenance Margin

This is the minimum value traders must keep in their trading account if they wish to keep a position open. The maintenance margin is usually lower compared to the initial margin.

Margin Call

If a trader's account falls short of the required maintenance margin, they receive a call from the brokerage firm, demanding to deposit the required amount. If a trader does not do so, the brokerage firm liquidates his positions amounting to the same value.

Market Order

An order to buy or sell any financial entity at the latest available price. Traders use this order when they want their trades to be executed quickly.

Market on Close

This order is used to buy or sell financial assets at the end of that trading session. The order price is typically within the closing range of market prices.

O

Offer Price

It shows the willingness of the seller to sell a financial asset at an agreed price. It is also called 'Ask' price.

Open Order

An order which is not executed. It can remain open till the specified price is reached or the order is canceled.

P

Pit

A specific place on the trading floor where traders conduct their buying and selling activities.

Position

A trade that has not been completed the process of both buying and selling. An open trade.

S

Settlement Price

This is the last price paid for any financial entity on a trading day. This is also called the closing price.

Scalp

A day trading method, where speculators trade for small profits. These trades are completed very quickly, within a few minutes. Scalpers trade multiple times through the same day.

Short

When a trader has a negative or bearish outlook on the market, he is said to be short on the market. Also, the selling side of an open derivative contract.

Speculator

Traders who try to anticipate market movements and price changes to earn profits.

Spot

Markets, where immediate delivery and cash payment is handled for financial assets.

Spread

Difference between the bid and ask price.

Stop Order

Also known as the stop-loss order. Traders use this order to limit the risk of loss or book profits at a certain price level.

Stop Limit

Like a stop order, but with a slight variation. Stop order with limit acts as a limit order in buying when the price is at or above the stop price. In selling, it becomes a limit order when the price is trading at or below the stock price.

T

Tick

In trading, the smallest increment in the price of any financial asset. Some scalpers use tick price for trading.

Conclusion

Day traders are technical traders. They rely on chart readings for executing their trades and ignore any other thing like the company's profitability, P/E ratio, debt-to-equity ratio, etc. For a day trader, technical charts are the only tools for making money. Usually, day trader's trade through a single session, and by the close of the day, they also close all open trades, not keeping any position open for the next day. Traders who keep their position open for the next session or overnight are swing traders.

A day trader can use many time frames on technical charts for trading. These time frames can range from one minute or lower to 5 minutes; 15 minutes; 30 minutes; 45 minutes; 1 hour; 4 hours; or even weekly and monthly. If you are wondering how day trader can use weekly or monthly charts, know the difference between using various time frames. Day traders decide their trading style by looking at the charts and deciding which time frame will suit them the most. Many day traders can spend hours in front of their computer screens every day. But several day traders trade only part-time, are busy with other jobs or work, and cannot spend much time trading every day. In such situations, these traders can study weekly or monthly charts and decide at what price level they will buy or sell any stock. After deciding that, they wait patiently for that level to arrive and trade only at then. There are many ways to set an alert to know when a price level has reached. The brokerage platforms have SMS facilities to alert their clients about stock prices. Mostly, charting software also has facilities to alert about a stock price level. By trading this way, they save precious time and money, which they can use for pursuing other money-making activities like a regular job or doing some other work.

There is another. Highly skilled type of day trading, call scalping. This is also known as micro-trading because the day trader focuses on a small timeframe (such as one minute or a few seconds) and trades for tiny profits. They keep the lot sizes higher so that small profits will also multiply into big money. Since the timeframe is very small, scalpers can trade several times throughout the day, sometimes even 20 to 50 times. But this is a risky type of trading and requires very fine trading skills. Otherwise, one can end up losing all the trading money within a single session.

Day trading is also about buying and selling on the same day. But compared to scalping, day traders have a bigger time frame for keeping their positions open. This can range from minutes to hours. The Internet is full of articles that portray glamorous pictures of day trading, making you believe that you can get rich quickly by this trading method. But this trading method requires hard work, knowledge, razor-sharp focus, and high levels of patience, not to mention a big chunk of money to invest in the early stages. If you are day trading, then you should be completely focused, you cannot allow yourself to be distracted by other things. If you can afford to have this kind of discipline and dedication, then you will find day trading suits you.

Another name for day trading is intraday trading. This term is a clearer definition of a day trader since it shows that buying and selling are happening within one day.

Day traders can develop their style into other types of trading, such as momentum trading, positional trading, swing trading, or long-term trading. All these styles are specialization forms of trading, but usually do not fall under the day trading category.

Printed in Great Britain
by Amazon